C000151349

Python for Beginners

Python for Beginners

Alex Bowers

LearnToProgram, Inc.
Vernon, Connecticut

LearnToProgram.tv, Incorporated
27 Hartford Turnpike Suite 206
Vernon, CT06066
contact@learntoprogram.tv
(860) 840-7090

©2013 by LearnToProgram.tv, Incorporated

ISBN-13: 978-0-9888429-7-7
ISBN-10: 0988842971

All rights reserved. No part of this document may be reproduced or
transmitted in any form or by any means, electronic, mechanical,
photocopying, recording, or otherwise, without prior written permission of
LearnToProgram.tv, Incorporated.

Limit of Liability/Disclaimer of Warranty: While the publisher and
author have used their best efforts in preparing this book, they make
no representations or warranties with respect to the accuracy or
completeness of the contents of this book and specifically disclaim any
implied warranties of merchantability or fitness for a particular purpose.
No warranty may be created or extended by sales representatives or
written sales materials. The advice and strategies contained herein may
not be suitable for your situation. You should consult with a professional
where appropriate. By following the instructions contained herein, the
reader willingly assumes all risks in connection with such instructions.
Neither the publisher nor author shall be liable for any loss of profit
or any other commercial damages, including but not limited to special,
incidental, consequential, exemplary, or other damages resulting in whole
or part, from the readers' use of, or reliance upon, this material.

Mark Lassoff, Publisher
Kevin Hernandez, VP/ Production
Alison Downs, Copy Editor
Alexandria O'Brien, Book Layout
Ardit Sulce, Technical Writer
Jeremias Jimenez, Technical Editor

Dedication

To the team at LearnToProgram: thank you for your trust and faith in me. Working alongside you has been incredible.

A special thank you to Mark for his guidance and assistance throughout the entire process.

Finally, a thank you to my parents, Caroline and Lee, and my brother Jonathan, for putting up with my seclusion while I harbored and honed my passion for programming.

TABLE OF CONTENTS

About the Author

Alex Bowers' programming career began when he learned PHP and
MySQL for a small project that he wanted to complete. Two years later,
the project was finished and Alex had become a bona fide PHP and
mySQL expert. He was hooked—he just couldn't get enough of coding!
This was the beginning of a lifelong passion for programming.

Since then, Alex has dedicated his time to teaching others. In 2009,
he began teaching PHP and MySQL on YouTube under the name
"TheTutSpace." He has since moved on to teach jQuery, Javascript and
HTML/CSS; manage a hugely successful forum, PHPacademy; and
author and produce content for various other educational sources all over
the web. Alex's primary expertise is in web development, but he has also
dabbled in Android and iOS.

Alex's style is very much compatible with LearnToProgram's mission:
to provide easy-to-access technical education for students worldwide.
For Alex, traditional classroom teaching is passé: his goal is to teach
thousands of students he has never met from all countries and cultures.

Courses Available from LearnToProgram, Inc.

AJAX Development
Android Development for Beginners
Become a Certified Web Developer
C Programming for Beginners
C# for Beginners
Creating an MP3 Player with Adobe Flash
CSS Development (with CSS3)
Design for Coders
HTML and CSS for Beginners (with HTML5)
HTML5 Mobile App Development with PhoneGap
iOS Development Code Camp
iOS Development for Beginners Featuring iOS5
iOS Development for Beginners Featuring iOS6/7
Java Programming for Beginners
Javascript for Beginners
jQuery for Beginners
Objective C for Beginners
Photoshop for Coders
PHP & MySQL for Beginners
Python for Beginners
SQL Database for Beginners
User Experience Design

Books from LearnToProgram, Inc.

HTML and CSS for Beginners
Javascript for Beginners
Create Your Own MP3 Player with HTML5

GETTING STARTED

CHAPTER OBJECTIVES:

• You will be able to set up the Python development environment.
• You will be able to set up Eclipse with PyDev as the platform where the Python code will be written.
• You will be able to write and run your first Python program.

1.1 ACQUIRING THE TOOLS

Before you begin working with and learning Python with this book, there are a few tools you will need. In this chapter, we will show you how to download and install the necessary tools: Python and Eclipse.

 Python is a remarkably powerful dynamic programming language that is used in a wide variety of application domains.

 Eclipse is a platform where you can write, edit, debug and run programming languages such as Python.

Before we can do anything, we need to set up our tools:

The first thing you will need is to install Python.

> **It can be downloaded for free from its official webpage at:**
> www.python.org/download

You will find many versions of Python in the "Download Python" section, but you should always use the current production version. Versions that are not yet in production may have undocumented errors, performance problems or other minor issues. At the time this book is being written, the current production versions are Python 2.7.4 and Python 3.3.1.

We are going to work with Python 3.3.1. It is both more secure and faster than its previous versions. The next step is to download one

**This book uses:
Python 3.3.1**

of the installers listed on the webpage. Which one you should choose depends on your operating system. As my operating system is the 64 bit version of Windows 7, I would download the Python 3.3.1 Windows X86-64 MSI Installer. Of course, you likely have a different combination of hardware and operating system. That's one of the nice things about Python—it runs on practically any hardware and operating system.

After the Python installer file has been downloaded, double-click on it and follow the prompts to install it.

Next, we'll set up the Eclipse IDE (Integrated Development Environment) where you can write, edit, debug and run the Python code.

> **Eclipse can be downloaded for free from its official webpage at:**
> www.eclipse.org/downloads

You will see many versions of Eclipse listed on the webpage. The one we are going to use throughout this book is Eclipse Standard (version 4.3 as of this writing) and also known as Eclipse Kepler. Once the file has been downloaded, double-click it to begin the installation. (You may need to extract the file from a compressed folder first.)

This book uses: Eclipse 4.3

In general, Eclipse is a well-supported platform and can be used on many operating systems. Eclipse is also designed to work with many different programming languages. I've used Eclipse for Java, PHP, and C++ development. Eclipse Classic will allow us to install an add-on so that we may use the Python interpreter within Eclipse.

Figure 1.1: The Eclipse executable appears in the extracted Eclipse folder downloaded from the website.

You might need the Java Runtime Environment installed on your system before installing Eclipse. If you don't have it, you will be prompted accordingly during the installation process.

If this is the case, you can download the Java Runtime Environment from:

Oracle's official Java site located at:
http://java.com/en/download/index.jsp

Tip: For Windows users, if you install the Eclipse IDE 32-bit version then you must install the Java Runtime Environment (JRE) 32-bit version. The same is true if you are installing 64-bit versions. Also, if you install Eclipse to, for example, folder C:\Eclipse, then you must override the default installation folder of the JRE and install the JRE to C:\Eclipse\jre because this is where the Eclipse IDE installation program will expect to find the Java Runtime Environment. You can go to: http://stackoverflow.com/questions/2030434/eclipse-no-java-jre-jdk-no-virtual-machine to view various user's comments and solutions to various problems you may encounter while installing the Eclipse IDE and the Java Runtime Environment for Windows.

After you have installed Eclipse and run it for the first time, you will see a window that looks like this:

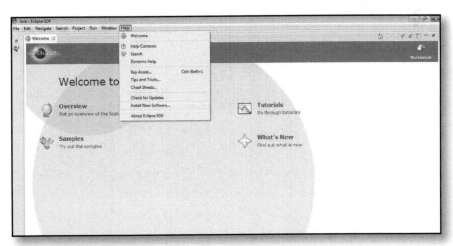

Figure 1.2: The Eclipse window opens after installation

From this window, go to *Help > Install New Software.*

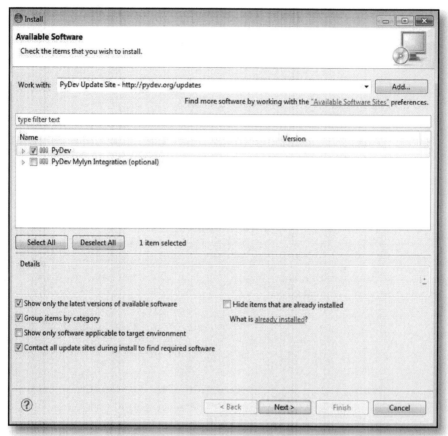

Figure 1.3: Installing the PyDev module

Inside the *Work with* box, type the address http://pydev.org/updates, which searches for the Python add-on for Eclipse. Hit *Enter* and then select *PyDev* from the returned results. Press *Next* until the installation is completed and accept any certificate you may be asked to during the installation. Choose to restart Eclipse at the end of the installation process.

When Eclipse restarts, it will ask you to choose a workspace. In order not to show this window the next time you open Eclipse, check the *Use this as a default and do not ask again* option.

The Eclipse window should now appear on your screen. We now will configure Eclipse to make it work with Python. This can be done by enabling the Python interpreter. To do this, go to *Window > Preferences* and expand *PyDev* as shown in the following image.

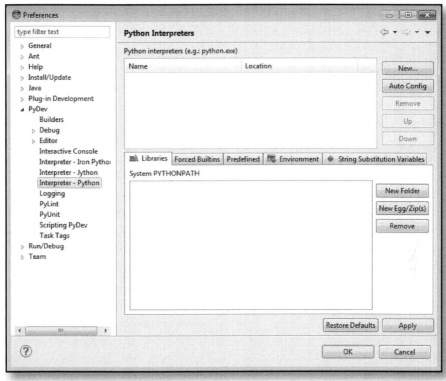

Figure 1.4: Enabling the Python interpreter

Now, we need to tell Eclipse where in the system the Python interpreter is located. To do this, go to the *New* button.

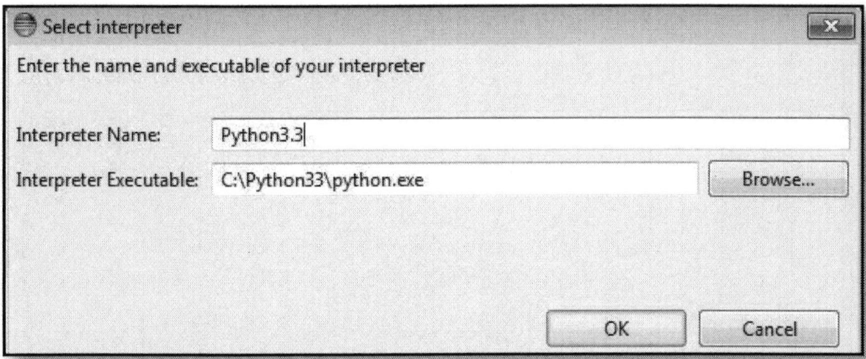

Figure 1.5: Setting the interpreter path

Type a name for the interpreter. It does not matter what name you choose but you should choose something relevant. I'm using *Python3.3*. Click *Browse* and locate the Python installation directory. Mine is located in C:\Python33. Find your Python executable file and click *Open* and then *OK* in the next window.

Now you are ready to start a new Python programming project inside the Eclipse platform. You can do that by going to *Project > New > PyDev Project*.

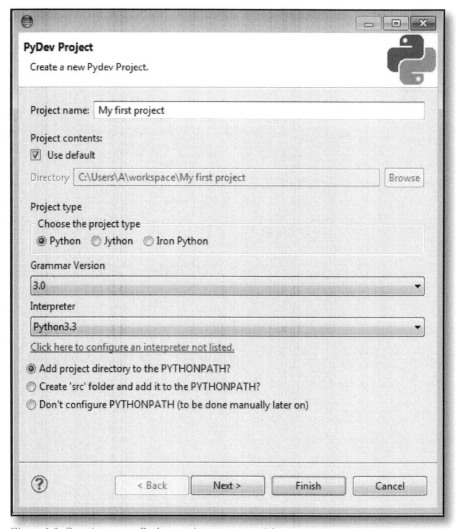

Figure 1.6: Creating a new Python project to start writing programs

Type a name for the project, change the *Grammar Version* to *3.0* and choose your Python interpreter from the *Interpreter* drop-down list. Mine would be *Python3.3* which is the interpreter name I created in the previous step.

Click *Next* and then *Finish* to close the window.

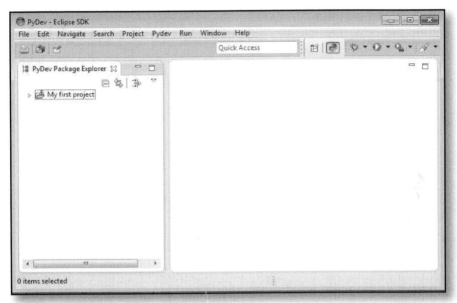

Figure 1.7: The project environment interface

You should now see the PyDev project environment with its Package Explorer window on the left-hand side as shown in the previous image.

1. Which of the following is needed to write and run a simple Python program such as the one created in this chapter?
   a. Java Runtime Environment.
   b. Eclipse.
   c. Python.
   d. Linux.

2. Which of the following statements is true?
   a. Python cannot work without Eclipse.
   b. Eclipse cannot work without Python.
   c. Eclipse is just an optional platform that helps users to work with Python.
   d. Python code can also be written somewhere else, but Eclipse is a necessity when the code has to be run/executed.

1.2 HELLO WORLD IN PYTHON

In this section, you will create your very first Python program. This simple program will display some text on the screen. Before going ahead and writing the Python code, we need to first create a folder and a file where we will write our script. To create a folder, from the *Package Explorer* tree view, right-click over the project and then go to *New > Folder* as shown in the following screenshot:

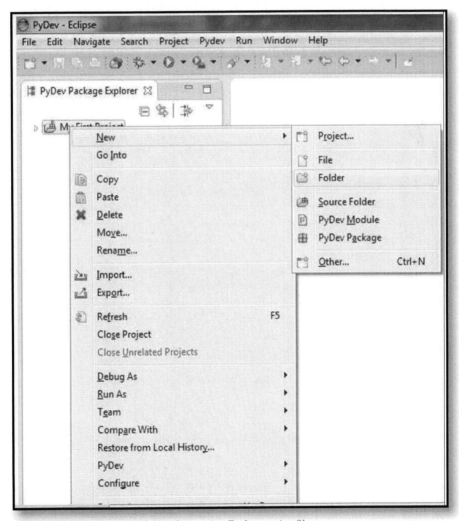

Figure 1.8: Creating a new folder for storing Python script files

> **Tip:** I'm using a PC to create this book, which is why all the screenshots are from Windows. Everything I am doing has an equivalent procedure on the Mac operating system. You can easily complete the book using a Mac—all the code will be identical.

Enter a name for the new folder and click *OK* to close the window. To create a file inside the folder, right-click the folder you created and go to *New > File*.

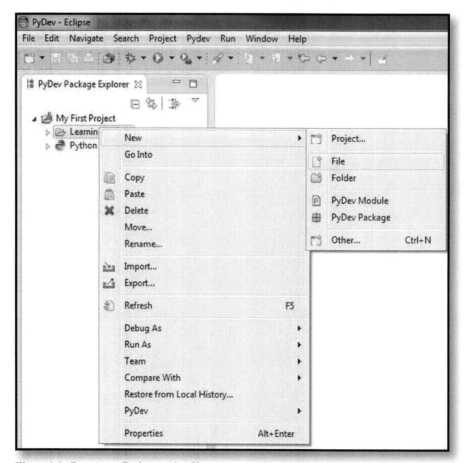

Figure 1.9: Creating a Python script file

Enter a name for the file. Since this is the file where we are going to write our first "Hello World" program, I will name mine "Hello.py" where "py" is the file extension indicating that particular file is a Python script. Once we have created our empty Python file, we can start coding right away. The area within the Eclipse environment where you are going to write the code is illustrated in the following image:

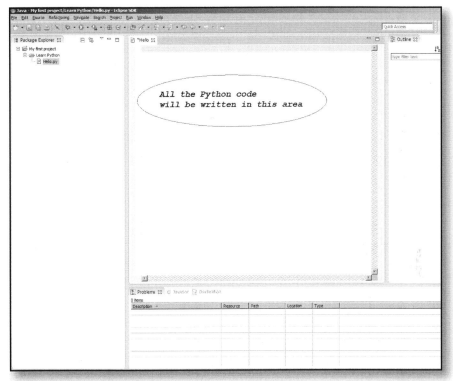

Figure 1.10: The programming environment

As we already mentioned, we are going to be creating a program that displays some text on the screen. In Python, this can easily be done using the **print** function. The whole code we need to write in the coding window is as follows:

```
print("Hello, world")
```

The *print* phrase is a Python keyword, which means it is a special word that is used and recognized by Python as a function. The quoted text— Hello, world—is the text we are actually going to output. Notice that it is surrounded by quotes and is known as a string.

After you write the code, you have to execute it in order to get the output you want. To execute the code, go to the *Run as* button from the icons menu and then to *Python run* and click *OK*. You should now see the output printed at the bottom of the window. In our case the output should be the text "Hello, world".

For Linux users, there is something else you have to do when writing Python code—you'll need to add an additional line before the code. A Python program that is meant to be run on a Linux machine would look like this:

```
#!/usr/local/bin/PythonDirectory
print("Hello, world")
```

The first line tells the interpreter where in your Linux machine the Python installation directory is located. This line is often referred to as the "Shebang line." (Bonus: it's fun to say "Shebang"!)

You've just created your first program, congratulations! We've kept it simple to start off with, but you now have the basic knowledge of where to write the code and how to run it in order to get your desired output. You'll be writing more complicated programs as we move on through the next chapters.

 QUESTIONS FOR REVIEW

1. What does the print command do?
   a. Initializes a Python program.
   b. Displays some text on the screen.
   c. Sends a command to the printer.
   d. None of the above.

2. What is not meant by "running the program"?
   a. Saving the written program inside Eclipse.
   b. Trying to get the output of the written program.
   c. Testing if the program is working.
   d. Executing the program.

CHAPTER 2

THE BASICS

CHAPTER OBJECTIVES

- You will be able to understand what variables do and learn how to assign values to them.
- You will be able to understand different data types and learn how to get the type of a specific variable or value.
- You will learn how to quickly test single lines of code without having to write the code inside Eclipse.
- You will learn to write simple arithmetic expressions, and learn the order of the arithmetic operations for complex expressions.
- You will learn how to insert comments inside your code.
- You will learn the scope of variables.

2.1 GETTING STARTED WITH VARIABLES

We can define variables as containers that are used to store data such as numbers, text, lists, and other similar objects. Variables are fundamental in every programming language as they give us a way to store and manipulate information as the program executes. As you practice using variables in this chapter, I am sure their application will become clearer.

> **Variables:**
> **Containers that are used to store data**

Before we start coding again, we need to create an empty Python file like we did when we created our first "Hello world" program. To create the file, right-click above the folder you created and stored your "Hello world" code in, and create a new file. I have named my file *Variables.py*.

Here is a first example of a variable with a sample value it might hold:

```
number =100
```

In this example we have assigned the value of 100 to the variable *number*. In other words, our container is now filled with the value of 100.

Note that the word *number* is just an arbitrary name we chose to give to our variable. You have a lot of freedom when writing variable names. However, there are a few things you should know about syntax rules of writing variables. You will see that some variable names are not allowed.

The following examples are correct variable name declarations in Python:	While the following names would not be allowed:
• number • Number • Number_1 • numberOne • _variableX • etc	• 1_number • +number • *number

As you can see, numbers and special characters (the only exception being the underscore) are not allowed to begin a variable name. Besides this important restriction, there is also a convention on Python variable names. The convention suggests that you use the camel casing method. In camel casing, you start your variable name with a lowercase letter and then you use capital letters if your variable name is longer than one word. Here are some examples:

Camel Casing Method

```
numberOne
thisIsAVariable
camelCasingWorks
```

Tip: While you have a lot of flexibility in how you name variables, it's important that you give the variables a name that has semantic meaning. Name variables based on what they are representing. If someone unfamiliar with your code were to read it, they should have some idea of what a variable represents, just by the name.

Let's take a look at a simple example of a variable in use in Python:

```
number = 100
print (number)
```

We just assigned a value to the variable *number* and then we displayed the variable value using the *print* command. After you run the code, you should get the value of 100 displayed on the screen.

If we modify the above code a bit, you will see a different result. When you see parentheses in Python code, work from the inside of the parentheses outward to interpret the code. In this case, we have embedded the *type()* function inside the print command and sent the value of the *number* variable as an argument to the function.

```
number = 100
print (type (number))
```

Running this code, you should get this result:

```
<class 'int'>
```

The result is declaring that the value of the variable is of the type *integer*. You will learn more about different data types in the next chapter.

> **Tip:** Variable names in Python are case-sensitive. The variable named "number", written in all lowercase letters, will be different from the variable named "Number", which has the first letter capitalized. If you assign a value of 100 to "number" and then try to retrieve that value from "Number", you will get an error.

2.2 Data Types

As is the case in many other computer programming languages, Python recognizes and works with several different types of data. In the previous chapter, we went through an example of viewing the data type of the variable *number*. The following code will also output the data type, but this time the result will indicate a floating point number:

```
number = 100.1
print (type (number))
```

Running this code, you should get this result:

Fig 2.1: Output of the type() method

In contrast to the value of 100 which was of type **integer**, in this case we are dealing with a **float** type. *Float* is an approximation of real numbers but does not include *integers* into its set. It is easiest to think of *floats* (floating point numbers) as numbers with a decimal value at the end. *Float* type values have a greater deal of precision than *integers*.

In Python it is possible to convert between different data types. This conversion process is frequently called **casting**. Examine the following code:

```
number = int(100.1)
print (type (number))
```

The result you get would be:

```
<class 'int'>
```

Look at the original assignment to the variable number. Before the value is actually assigned, the int() function is used to convert the value to an integer. When the conversion occurs, the level of precision is reduced and, effectively, the decimal part of the number is dropped. Since the casting has taken place before the value is assigned to *number*, the type() function now yields *int* or integer type.

Let's alter the code again and see what happens:

```
number = int(100.1)
print (number)
```

The value displayed on the screen when the program is run is 100 instead of 100.1. If we want to make the previous code more compact and have it display both the converted value and its type at the same time, we would write:

```
number = int(100.1)
print (type(number),number)
```

When run, this code would yield the following result:

```
<class 'int'> 100
```

Variables don't always get assigned numbers as values. Variables may also contain strings, lists, tuples or dictionaries. Here is an example of a variable that is assigned a **string** value:

```
a = "This is a string"
print (type(a),a)
```

The output would be:

```
<class'str'> This is a string
```

The result of the type() function, *Str,* indicates that the value inside the variable *a* is of type *string*. You can think of a string as a series of characters. The characters included in a string can be letters, numbers or punctuation marks. When the string is defined we surround it with double quotes to demarcate the beginning and end of the string.

If we wanted to write our sentence on more than one line, the approach would be as follows:

```
a =   """ This is
a string """
print (a)
```

or, alternatively:

```
a = "This is \na string"
print (a)
```

Running the last two examples would yield similar results. In the first example, the use of triple quotes allows the expansion of the text in more than one line. In the second example, the characters **\n** do the work of shifting the characters to the second line and can be considered a reserved word in Python. *Print* is another example of a reserved word. \n is very flexible as it can be written directly next to strings without having to add a space, as shown previously. If you found yourself in a situation where you would have to display the \n character as printed text for some reason, you would write:

> A reserved word is a word that is part of the programming language and performs an assigned action.

```
a = "This is \\na string"
print (a)
```

In this case, the \n part would not be recognized as a reserved word anymore. The preceding slash is said to 'escape' the character sequence.

Take a look at the following code, paying special attention to variables *a* and *b*:

```
a = "Hello"
b = "%s world" % a
print (b)
```

The output of this code is simply:

```
Hello world
```

%s and **%** are both reserved words. *%s* is a container that is waiting to be filled with a value. Then, the character % indicates that the container *%s* should be filled with the value of variable *a*. You will realize later that these containers will come to be very useful when formatting complex strings. If you are familiar with C style languages, you have likely seen this concept before where character sequences such as %s are used to output variable values.

We could also create the same output in another way:

```
a = "Hello"
b = "{} world".format(a)
print (b)
```

In the code above, we assign the string value to variable *a* in the first line. Then, in the second line we are dealing with a string method which is *str.format()*. This method replaces the *ß* part with the value assigned to *a*. The output is then printed in the last line.
So far, we have worked numbers (integers and floats) and strings in terms of data types. Now, we are going to learn two other important data types: **tuples** and **lists**.

This would be a *tuple*:

```
X = (1,2,3)
```

and this would be a *list*:

```
Y = [1,2,3]
```

To get the types of *X* and *Y*, you can use the *type()* function similar to how you used it with numbers and strings:

```
type (X)
type (Y)
```

Even though the *tuple* and the *list* look similar to each other, they are designed to deal with different tasks. Lists are mutable (changeable) while tuples are immutable (not changeable). We can add, modify or remove elements from lists, but we cannot do the same with tuples. Tuples are designed only to store data. To illustrate the mutability of lists, we will add an element to our existing list, *Y*:

Lists: mutable

Tuples: immutable

```
Y = [1,2,3]
Y.append(4)
print (Y)
```

If you run this short program, the result you will get is:

```
[1,2,3,4]
```

If you were to try the append() function with the *tuple* in the same way, you would get an error:

```
Test.py ✕
    Y = (1,2,3)
    Y.append(4)
    print (Y)




    ◀

Console ✕   PyUnit                                                    ■
<terminated> C:\Users\A\workspace\My first project\Sc.py
Traceback (most recent call last):
  File "C:\Users\A\workspace\My first project\Sc.py", line 2, in <module>
    Y.append(4)
AttributeError: 'tuple' object has no attribute 'append'
```

Figure 2.2: Python responds with an error when the append() method is applied to a tuple

The append method tries to mutate the tuple—which is not allowed since tuples are by definition immutable.

In addition to using append() to modify a list, you might also want to access certain elements within a *list* or a *tuple*. Let's say we want to print out the third element of the list *X*.

```
X = [1,2,3]
print (X[2])
```

Executing the code above, you would display the value 3 because it is the third member of the list. *X[2]*, within the print() function picks the third element of the list. You might expect *X[3]* to select the third member of the list, however, in Python, indexing begins at zero. This means any object that holds a list of subsequent values will enumerate the first value as zero. So, if we wanted to display the first element from the list, we would write:

```
X = [1,2,3]
print (X[0])
```

We can use the same notation to extract a range of numbers within the list, for example, if we wanted to extract the third, fourth, and fifth values we could write the following code:

```
X = ["a","b","c","d","e","f"]
print (X[2:5])
```

When executed, this code would yield the result:

```
['c','d','e']
```

These are the elements with index 2, 3, and 4, respectively. Notice that when we request the list values 2:5, we don't receive the fifth value. The return stops before the second value in the request. 5:7 would return elements with indexes 5 and 6. Similarly, just as we just did with lists, we can access elements from tuples:

```
Y = (1,2,3,4,5,6)
print (X[2:5])
```

Now that you understand a bit about lists and tuples, we are going to learn another important data type, **dictionaries**. *Dictionaries* also store multiple elements as *lists* and *tuples* do, but with the difference that these elements are stored in key/value pairs. Here is an example of a *dictionary* that stores a list of names and phone numbers:

Dictionaries

```
D = {"Tim": 981244, "Tom": 897134, "John": 
9809878}
```

The first element of each pair is called the **key**, while the second is the **value**. Each *value* is tied to its *key*. If we want to know Tom's phone number, we would write:

```
D["Tom"]
```

We would get Tom's phone number displayed on the screen. In addition to the curly bracket syntax that you saw in the first example, *dictionaries* can also be declared in another way:

```
D =  dict ( Tim = 981244, Tom = 897134, 
John = 9809878)
```

Regardless of the declaration method, the result would be the same. We could access any value in the dictionary using the notation above, regardless of how the dictionary was created.

Booleans are another important data type. Booleans may contain only two values, **True** or **False**. Try entering and running the following code to get the idea:

Booleans

```
Freedom = True
print (type (Freedom))
```

What you get as a result is this:

```
<class 'bool'>
```

Where *bool* indicates that *True* is of type *Boolean*.
Next try running the following code to see what it does:

```
a, b = 0, 1
if a == b:
    print (True)
else:
    print (False)
```

In the first line of code above, we are assigning a value of zero for
variable *a,* and a value of 1 for variable *b*. The remaining block of code is
a conditional expression where we test if *a* is equal to *b*. If they are equal,
True will be displayed on the screen, otherwise *False* will be displayed. In
this case, the result would be:

```
False
```

The double equal sign "==" is a comparison operator that means
equivalency.

> **Tip:** A common mistake made by those learning to program is
> to confuse the = and the == operator. (Just be thankful Python
> doesn't have a === operator, like Javascript does!) Remember that
> = is the assignment operator used to assign a value to a variable.
> The == operator is a comparison operator used to compare two
> values.

Try to carefully observe the syntax and the structure of the code block.
Besides the usage of columns which are easily visible, you can also
see that we have shifted two of the lines to the right. This is called
indentation and it is very important in Python. Statements such as
print should be indented in the code when being used inside blocks
such as conditionals. You will learn more about indentation in the next
chapters.

2.3 ARITHMETIC OPERATORS

Until now, we have been writing our Python code examples inside Eclipse. Now, it is time to try a slightly different way of writing and running the code. In programming terminology, this is known as the **interactive way** and it is generally done through the command line of the operating system you are using.

Windows users will have to open the Command Prompt from the Start menu. Linux and Mac users would open the Terminal. After you have opened the command line specific to your system, type in *python* and hit enter. You should come up with something like this:

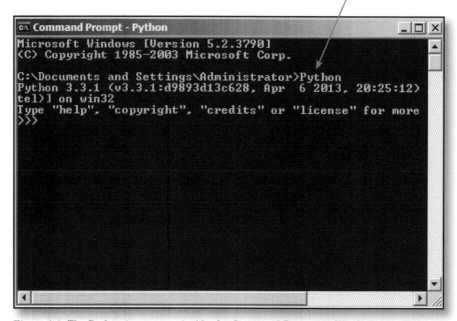

Figure 2.3: The Python interpreter inside the Command Prompt in Windows

This window shows the interactive programming environment. This method is primarily used for testing small single lines of code instead of big blocks. Try this code inside the window and hit enter:

```
1+2
```

You just wrote and ran a line of code at the same time using only a few clicks. However, notice that we are not saving the code inside a file as we did in Eclipse, meaning that this method is just for testing purposes.

In the previous code you wrote an expression that contains a mathematical operator (the addition operator (+)). Similarly, you can try all other types of operators you have learned from mathematics such as multiplication:

```
1*2
```

division:

```
1/2
```

Or exponentiation:

```
1**2
```

Try to understand what the following code does by observing its output:

```
round (3/4)
```

The program first divides four by three, and then rounds up the output value to the nearest integer. To make things a bit more complex, try this other expression which involves the modulus operator (%). The modulus operator returns the remainder of the division.

```
round ((3/4)  *  (10%3))
```

In terms of its output, the expression above would be the same as:

```
round (0.75  *  1)
```

or:

```
round (0.75)
```

and the result would be zero in all three cases.

2.4 Understanding the Order of the Operators

When using operators in expressions that involve more than one operator, certain rules should be followed in terms of arithmetic operation order. These rules are basically the same as in mathematics. Try to rewrite the expression we used in section 2.3, but this time without some of the parentheses:

```
round (3/4 * 10%3)
```

You will see that the result would be different. When you don't use brackets, the default operator execution order is applied to expression. Therefore, you should always use brackets inside the sub-expressions to tell the program how your operations are grouped:

```
round ((3/4) * (10%3))
```

Here is a simpler example:

```
1-2*3
```

Some would expect that the first operator (-) is executed first and therefore, the output would be a value of "3", but this is not true. As in mathematics, the multiplication would be the first to be executed. If you want the subtraction operator as the first operator, then you would have to write:

```
(1-2) * 3
```

To sum it up, if you don't use brackets, the default operation order will be applied to your expression, which is: exponents and roots, multiplication and division (performing whichever operation appears first from left to right), and last addition and subtraction (again, performing whichever comes first from left to right).

2.5 COMMENTS

So far we have written code that is **executable**, meaning that the code does something and gives an output while being run. We can also write code or descriptive text that we don't want to be executed, but instead be ignored. This kind of text is referred to as **comments**. *Comments* can serve either as descriptive text, as code that we don't want to execute, or as code we want to execute at some later point. Try this example in Eclipse and see what output you get:

```
# print ("Hello world")
print ("Hello")
```

The first line is what we referred to as a *comment* while the second line is normal code that does something when the code is executed. You can see that we had to start with the "#" symbol to declare that we are actually commenting instead of coding. If we want to run the first line of code, we can simply remove the "#" symbol.
Another scenario where commenting would become useful is when we want to describe what our code does:

```
print ("Hello world") # This code displays
the text inside the brackets
```

Describing what the code does might come in handy when we want to give the code to someone else or even when we work with our code at a later time.

Executable Code	Comments Code
Active output when ran	Nonexecutable descriptions

2.6 VARIABLE SCOPE

We have learned quite a few things about variables, such as what they are for and how to assign values to them. A concept that you should also know is the scope of the variables inside a Python program. The variable scope is a concept that tightly relates to functions, which are used to perform some actions and return an output, pretty much the same as functions in math do. Functions can have variables within them. When variables are declared outside the function body, the variables are called **global**, while if the variables are declared inside the function, they are called **local**. *Global* variables can be accessed both outside and inside the functions while *local* variables can only be accessed inside the functions they are declared in.

> **Global Variables:**
> declared outside the function body
>
> **Local Variables:**
> declared inside the function body

To illustrate what we just stated, try to understand and run the following example in Eclipse or in your Python command line:

```
def f(x):
    y = x**2
    print y
print f(3)
print y
print x
```

In this code we create a function that calculates and prints out the square of a number. Two variables (x and y) are declared inside the function. Both are *local* variables. In line 4 we are printing out the output of the function when the input is equal to 3.

If we try to access these variables outside the function, as we are doing in the previous code in the two last lines with the print commands, we will be prompted that these objects are not defined and not recognized as variables by Python. You will learn more about variables and the usefulness of functions as we move on.

QUESTIONS FOR REVIEW

1. Let's say we have assigned a value to variable *a* as *a = 1*
Which of the following codes would print out the variable's assigned value?
   a. print ("a")
   b. display (a)
   c. print (a)
   d. print "a"

2. Which of the following is not a data type in Python?
   a. String.
   b. Decimal.
   c. Integer.
   d. Float.

3. Which of the following is not a correct declaration in Python?
   a. a = [1,2,3]
   b. b= {1,2,3}
   c. c = (1,2,3)
   d. d = "d"

4. Which of the following would be a correct order of execution of arithmetic operators, assuming there are no parentheses in the expression?
   a. Exponents, addition, division.
   b. Roots, multiplication, addition.
   c. Exponents, multiplication, roots.
   d. Addition, subtraction, division.

5. What is not true about comments?
   a. Comments are lines of code that automatically generate descriptions.
   b. Comments help the programmer keep track of the code by describing it.
   c. Comments are lines of code that are not executed by the program.
   d. Comments may be used as code that can be executed at a later time.

Using the following equation, let's figure out the acceleration of a vehicle in motion.

$$v = u + at$$

Where v is final velocity (25m/s), u is initial velocity (0 m/s) and t is time taken (10 seconds).

Work out acceleration (a) and print it to the screen

Hint: Rearrange it, like so:

$$a = \frac{u - v}{t}$$

LAB SOLUTION

```
a = 0
u = 0
v = 25
t = 10

a = (v - u) / t

print(a)
```

Chapter 2 Summary

In this chapter you were introduced to variables and we discussed how to write them and how to assign values to them.

You learned the concept of data types and what data types are available. You were also introduced to the basic syntax of assigning values of different data types to variables.

Together with variables and data types, you were provided with examples of basic mathematical operators and the rules of writing them in the correct order.

You should been able to understand the usefulness of writing comments and how to insert them into your code. You should now know that comments can be written either for documenting your code or for creating code that is to be executed at a later point.

Lastly, you gained a basic understanding of the variable scope concept. You learned that the scope of the variables is either local or global and you should understand what each of those terms mean.

In chapter 3, you will be introduced to conditionals which are a very important part of every programming language and allow the performance of multiple actions depending on a wide range of conditions.

Python for Beginners

CHAPTER 3

CONDITIONALS

CHAPTER OBJECTIVES

- You will be able to use conditionals including *if, elif, else* and *inlineif* statements.
- You will learn which statement to use depending on the scenario.
- You will learn a workaround of switch statements.
- You will be able to write conditionals on only one line using the *inline if* statements.

3.1 IF STATEMENTS

In this chapter you will be learning about conditionals which are used widely in every programming language.

 Conditionals are statements that perform actions depending on whether a condition evaluates as true or false. Here is an example of a conditional statement:

```
a, b = 0, 1
if a == b:
    print (True)
```

In the previous example, we are first assigning 0 and 1 to *a* and *b*, respectively, and then we write the condition statement in the second line (i.e. "if *a* is equal to *b*"). The third line contains the action to be performed if the condition in the second line is met. You will not get any result from this code because in this case, the condition is not met—*a* is not equal to *b*. So, nothing will happen. If we instead write:

```
a, b = 0, 1
if not a == b:
    print (True)
```

The output would be:

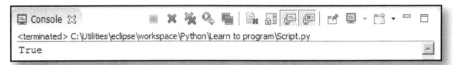

Figure 3.1: *True* is printed out because *a* is not equal to *b*

This is because the condition states that *a* is not equal to *b*, which is actually true.

Similarly, instead of the equal operator "==" you can try other operators inside the condition statement such as the comparison operators, >, <, <=, etc. Here is an example of how you would use the "less than or equal to" (<=) operator:

```
a, b = 0, 1
if a <= b:
    print ("Yes, a is equal or less than b")
```

This would give:

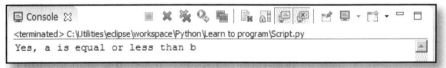

Figure 3.2: Text is printed out because the condition is met

Notice how the action to be performed (i.e. the *print* function) is indented. How much it is indented it does not matter, but it should not be at the same vertical alignment with the condition above.

Indentation is an integral part of conditional   **Indentation**
blocks. You should always indent the code that
comes under the conditional statements, just as we did in the previous code. Keeping this in mind, let's try some more complex conditions. We will write the previous code in another way and still get the same result by using a **bitwise operator.**

Bitwise operators allow the evaluation and manipulation of two or more input and are often used together with conditionals. **Or** is an example of a *bitwise operator*.   **Or**
It is used to evaluate if at least one input is true.

Here is an example:

```
a, b = 0, 1
if a < b or a == b:
    print ("Yes, a is equal or less than b")
```

We could translate the second and the third lines into common language in this way: "if *a* is either less than or equal to *b*, then print out the text '*Yes, a is equal to or less than b*'", which is actually true in our case. Therefore, the output would be:

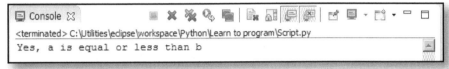

Figure 3.3: Text is printed out as *a* is less than *b*

Another important *bitwise operator* is **and**. The *and* operator evaluates the condition by only performing the succeeding action if both the conditions before and after *and* are true. Here is an example:

> **And**

```
a, b = 0, 1
if a < b and a == b:
    print ("Yes, a is equal or less than b")
```

We would read the code this way: "if *a* is at the same time less than and equal to *b*, then print out the text '*Yes, a is equal to or less than b*'", which is not true in our case. Therefore, nothing would be printed out this time.

> Please note the difference between the assign operator "=" and the equal operator "==". The former is used to assign values to variables, while the latter is usually used for testing if something is equal to something else.

> **Bitwise Operators:**
> • **Or**
> • **And**

3.2 ELSE STATEMENTS

You might have noticed that when we ran the following code:

```
a, b = 0, 1
if a == b:
    print (True)
```

Nothing happened, nothing was printed out. This is because the condition in the second line was not met—*a* was not equal to *b*. We might find it useful to also trigger an action when the condition is not met. This is done through the **else** statement which is written in the same structure inside the block as the *if* statement:

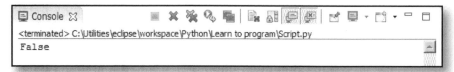

```
a, b = 0, 1
if a == b:
    print (True)
else:
    print (False)
```

In this case we would get *False* printed out:

```
Console ⊠                                               □
<terminated> C:\Utilities\eclipse\workspace\Python\Learn to program\Script.py
False
```

Figure 3.4: *False* is printed out as part of the *else* clause

The *else* statement and its consequent action are properly indented and aligned with the upper part of the conditional block, similar to the *if* statement. Notice that the indentation before the first and the second *print* has to be in the same amount. For example, if you used a four space indentation for the first *print* command, you have to use the same amount for the second one.

3.3 ELIF STATEMENTS

So far, we have tested two condition scenarios, *true* and *false*. Sometimes it becomes necessary to test multiple scenarios and perform actions depending on whether each of the conditions are met or not. Testing more than two conditions using the *if* and *else* statements is not possible—this is where the **elif** statement comes in. The *elif* statement is the abbreviation of "else if" and is used to state a condition just like the *if* statement does. The difference here is that the *elif* statement can be used multiple times inside a single conditional block. Here is an example:

```python
a, b = 0, 1
if a == b:
    print ("a is equal to b")
elif a  < b:
    print ("a is less than b")
elif a  > b:
    print ("a is less than b")

else:
    print ("a is greater than b")
```

You can include as many **elif** statements as you need inside the conditional block depending on your needs. In the previous code, the text that will be printed out is the one that meets the condition (i.e. $a < b$):

Figure 3.5: Text is printed out as part of an *elif* clause

Try to play around by changing the values of a and b in the first line and see what output you get. For example, if we assign 1 to both a and b:

```python
a, b = 1, 1
if a == b:
    print ("a is equal to b")
```

```
elif a < b:
    print ("a is less than b")
elif a > b:
    print ("a is less than b")
else:
    print ("a is greater than b")
```

We would get the first condition returned as true and therefore the following text printed out:

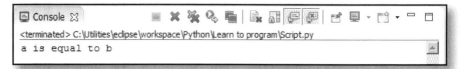

Also keep in mind that if none of the *if* or *elif* conditions are met, the action under *else* will be the one that is performed.

3.4 SWITCH STATEMENTS WORKAROUND

Many languages have a functionality called **switch statements**.

Switch statements are used to test multiple conditions and perform actions depending on them—the same thing that *elif* does. However, Python does not have built-in *switch statement* functionality, but it does have an easy workaround to that.

To illustrate the workaround of *switch statements*, we are going to create a dictionary:

Switch

```
a = dict (
    one = 1,
    two  =  2,
    three =  3
)
var = "two"
print (a[var])
```

The output of this code would be:

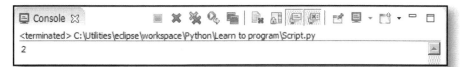

Figure 3.7: "2" is printed out as the value of variable "two"

This is because 2 is the value that is tied to key *two* which is assigned to the variable *var*. If you assign "four" to the variable, you will get an error because there is no "four" key in the dictionary.

Another slightly different workaround to the *switch* method is to use the built-in **get** function: This function returns a value for a given key.

Get

```
a = dict (
    one = 1,
    two  =  2,
    three =  3
```

```
)
var = "two"
print (a.get(var, "default"))
```

This code would print out the value that the key assigned to variable *var* holds in the case when this key exists in the dictionary. Otherwise, "default" will be printed out. In this case, we would get:

Figure 3.8: "2" is printed out instead of "default"

If we assign to *var* a value other than the ones contained in the dictionary:

```
a = dict (
    one = 1,
    two  =  2,
    three =  3
)
var = "six"
print (a.get(var, "default"))
```

we would get:

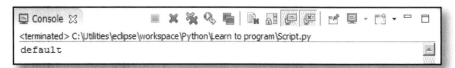

Figure 3.9: "default" is printed out, as "six" does not exist in the dictionary

There is a lot of freedom for you to choose between working with elif statements or using the switch statement workaround. However, these were two examples that can be used as quick workarounds for the switch method in Python in case you don't want to use elif statements.

3.5 INLINE IF

In addition to the conditional blocks we previously learned, there is also another quicker way of writing conditions. This is known as **inline if**. In this case, the condition and the action are both written in one line:

Inline If

```
a, b = 0, 1
print (True if a == b else False)
```

This means that *True* will be printed if *a* is equal to *b*, otherwise *False* will be displayed. In this case, the output would be:

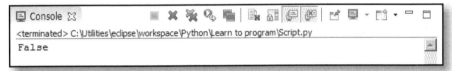

Figure 3.10: *True* is printed out as part of the *if* clause inside the *inline if* statement

Similarly, you can include other types of expressions inside the *inline if* and even assign the whole line to a variable:

```
a, b = 0, 1
var = "This is true" if a == b else "This
is not true"
print (var)
```

The output of this is:

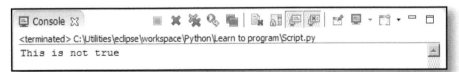

Figure 3.11: Text is printed out as part of the *else* clause inside the *inline if* statement

The last code is a very commonly used case of the *inline if* functionality as it allows variables to be assigned values depending on the conditions. However, the *inline if* conditionals are restricted, meaning that they cannot be used in complex expressions. When complex expressions are concerned, the standard *if, else* and *elif* statements, which you learned in the previous sections, should be used. The multiline structure of the standard conditionals allows us to write more advanced programs that have conditional aspects at the core.

QUESTIONS FOR REVIEW

1. Which of the following is a correctly written expression?
    a. if a = b:
    print ("Yes")
    b. if a == b:
    print("Yes")
    c. if a == b
       print("Yes")
    d. if a == b:
       print(Yes)

2. What is not true about elif?
    a. Elif is used when testing multiple statements.
    b. Elif is a substitute of the switch function.
    c. Elif is similar to the switch workaround method.
    d. Elif initiates a condition, similar to how *if* does.

3. What happens when none of the conditions are true in a conditional block?
    a. The action under else is executed.
    b. Nothing happens.
    c. The program throws an error.
    d. False is printed out.

4. How would you write a code that prints "Greater" if *a* is greater than *b*, and "Less or equal" if *a* is less than or equal to *b*, using the *inline if* statement?
    a. a, b = 10, 20
    print ("Greater" if a < b else "Less or equal")
    b. a, b = 10, 20
    print ("Greater" if a > b elif"Less or equal")
    c. a, b = 10, 20
    print ("Less or equal" if a <= b else "Greater")
    d. a, b = 10, 20
    print ("Greater" if a >= b else "Less or equal")

CHAPTER 3 LAB EXERCISE

One key thing about conditional statements is their ability to create something called a **truth table** which holds a certain number of input (usually a minimum of two) with one exception –*not*. *Truth tables* run using binary, which is what is happening behind the scenes within Python. Your input is being converted to binary when you are doing a comparison. There are six *truth tables* in total, however, we will only be looking at three of them, *And, Or* and *Not*.

Take the following tables and try to convert them into *if statements* in order to receive the correct output. Each row shows a different set of input:

AND
```
|-----------|
| A | B | Q |
|-----------
| 1 | 1 | 1 |
| 0 | 0 | 0 |
| 1 | 0 | 0 |
| 0 | 1 | 0 |
|----------|
```

You can see that the only place where two 'true' statements get passed is 1 and 1. This is the only output which is true, the rest being false.

The next two *truth tables* are as follows:

OR
```
|-----------|
| A | B | Q |
|----------
| 1 | 1 | 1 |
| 0 | 0 | 0 |
| 1 | 0 | 1 |
| 0 | 1 | 1 |
|----------|
```

As you can see with *OR*, any case having at least one 1 is true. Try to represent this using *if* statements as well.

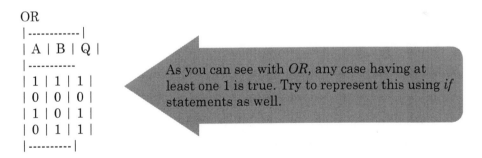

In this case I would utilize the *and* operator in Python to show you exactly what is happening behind the scenes for the *or* truth table. Python also has this built-in using the *or* operator. We can use this functionality later on to save us from having to write unnecessary code.

NOT
```
|--------|
| A | Q |
|--------|
| 1 | 0 |
| 0 | 1 |
|--------|
```

As you can see with *not*, it is the exception that takes only one input. The way this works is that it basically reverses the values.

Now for the real challenge! Try to write the code for the following truth table.

The equation for this truth table is as follows:

A *and not* B or C = Q

The equation is read from left to right and would appear like this if written in mathematical terms:

$((A \& \sim B) | C) = Q$

Using the above tables, create a program that will give you the correct output for the following table:

```
|---------------|
| A | B | C | Q |
|---------------|
| 1 | 1 | 1 |   |
| 1 | 0 | 1 |   |
| 1 | 1 | 0 |   |
| 1 | 0 | 0 |   |
| 0 | 1 | 0 |   |
| 0 | 0 | 1 |   |
| 0 | 0 | 0 |   |
| 0 | 1 | 1 |   |
|-------------|
```

Good luck!

Note: The creation of the main challenge will involve using more variables to store the current details in than shown above.

LAB SOLUTION

AND TRUTH TABLE:

```
a = 1
b = 0
if (a == 1 and b == 1):
print('1')
elif ((a == 1 and b == 0) or (a == 0 and b
== 1)):
print('0')
elif (a == 0 and b ==0):
print('0')
else:
print('Invalid Input')
```

OR TRUTH TABLE:

```
a = 1
b = 0
if (a == 1 and b == 1):
print('1')
elif ((a == 1 and b == 0) or (a == 0 and b
== 1)):
print('1')
elif (a == 0 and b ==0):
print('0')
else:
print('Invalid Input')
```

NOT TRUTH TABLE:

```python
a = 0
if(a == 1):
print('0')
elif(a == 0):
print('1')
else:
print('Invalid Input')
```

MAIN CHALLENGE:

```python
a = 1
b = 0
c = 1

if(b == 1):
bHolder = 0
elif(b==0):
bHolder = 1

if(a == 1 and bHolder == 1):
firstBracketHolder = 1
else:
firstBracketHolder = 0
if(firstBracketHolder == 1 or c == 1):
print('Q = 1')
else:
print('Q = 0')
```

CHAPTER 3 SUMMARY

In this chapter you were introduced to conditionals, which are a very important part of every programming language as they allow conditioned programming.

We discussed how useful the *if* statement is when you want to perform an action that is dependent on a certain condition. Along with the *if* statement, you learned that the code block preceding the *if* statement should be properly indented.

You experimented with the *else* statement and understood that it can be used as an alternative condition when the *if* statement is not satisfied.

You performed multiple actions that were dependent on multiple conditions made possible by the *elif* statement.

We also discussed an alternative workaround of the *switch* statements used in other programming languages. You should know that the *switch* workaround is also an alternative to the *elif* statements.

Lastly, you worked out another quick way of building *if* statements using the *inline if* alternative which, even though it is more restricted in terms of the complexity of actions it can perform, can be a quicker solution on certain occasions.

In the next chapter you will be introduced to the **looping** concept. Looping is crucial when working with large amounts of data. Basically, *looping* is used to run repetitive actions until a condition is specified. It has a number of methods which you will learn throughout the chapter.

CHAPTER 4

LOOPING

CHAPTER OBJECTIVES

- You will be introduced to types of looping, including *while* loops and *for* loops.
- You will learn more advanced functionalities to control flow.
- You will be introduced to the error handling issues and methods for efficient spotting and displaying of occurring errors.

4.1 WHILE LOOPS

 While loops are a type of looping in Python. They are a tool that enables the performing of repetitive actions until a certain condition is met. You can think of them as repeating *if* statements. Here is an example of a *while* loop:

While

```
a = 0
while a < 100:
    print (a)
    a += 1
```

Tip: += in the fourth line of the sample code above is known as the **Add and Assignment** operator. It will add 1 to the current value of **a** and then replace **a** with this new value.

Try to run the previous code in Eclipse. You will get a list of numbers from zero to 99, partially shown in the following output screenshot:

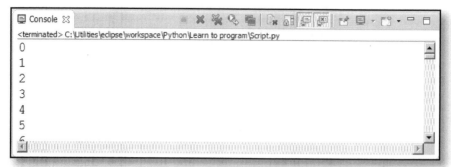

```
Console ⊠                                    ✕ ⚒ ⚒ ⬚ ⬚ | ⬚ ⬚ ⬚ ⬚ ⬚ | ⬚ ⬚ ▾ ⬚ ▾ ⬚ ⬚
<terminated> C:\Utilities\eclipse\workspace\Python\Learn to program\Script.py
0
1
2
3
4
5
6
```

Figure 4.1: Generated numbers from zero to 99 (shown up to five in the screenshot)

In the previous example, we started writing our code by assigning an initial value of zero to variable *a* in the first line. The rest of the code belongs to the *while* loop block. The first line of the *while* block makes up the condition of the block which states that *a* should not go higher than 100. If the enumeration reaches 100, the action (i.e. printing out) will stop.

The second line of the *while* block is the action, which orders the printing out of the value of *a*. The third line of the block declares the iteration **step.**

Step

A step is the interval used by the loop to iterate through a range or a set of numbers. In this case, the step is one, meaning that the iteration would start from zero, go to one, two and up to **99**, incrementing by one each time. In each pass, the value of *a* will be printed out, that is 0, 1, and so on. You might also come upon cases when a step other than one will be used.

To understand the previous code better, we will translate it into common language like so: Print out the value of *a* starting from zero (*a = 0*) and keep printing by incrementing upwards by one (*a +=1*). Do the printing out as long as *a* is less than 100 (while a < 100), and stop when the number has reached 100. When the loop reaches the limit, it is referred to as exhaustion of the loop.

You could also try a more simple code that prints out text instead of numbers:

```
a = 0
while a < 100:
    print ("Hello, world")
    a +=1
```

This time we are repeatedly printing out some text until it reaches the value of 100:

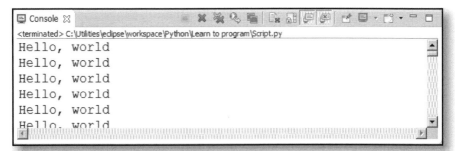

Figure 4.2: Text printed out 99 times until the loop is exhausted.

> **Tip:** In the previous examples we used a step of one to iterate from zero to 100. You can always use different steps and different ranges for iterating.

Please notice that the lines under the *while* statement are indented with the same amount of white space. The same amount of indentation indicates that we are still inside the *while* loop block. If we want to perform an action outside the *while* loop block, we would use a different amount of indentation. Here is an example:

```
a = 0
while a < 100:
    print ("Hello, world")
    a +=1
print ("The end")
```

> **Tip:** Keep in mind that the program interpreter executes the code block by block, starting at the top and moving down. In the previous example we have three blocks: the variable declaration block, the *while* loop block, and the *print* block. The *print* block will be executed only after the execution of the upper blocks has finished. Therefore, the output of the last block will be displayed at the very bottom of the output window.

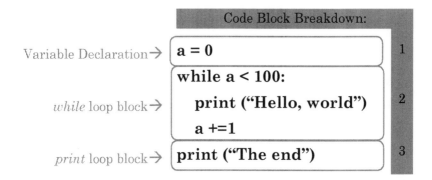

Code Block Breakdown:

Variable Declaration→

```
a = 0
```
1

while loop block→

```
while a < 100:
    print ("Hello, world")
    a +=1
```
2

print loop block→

```
print ("The end")
```
3

Here is the output:

```
Console 🔲                                    🔲 ✖ 🔲 🔲 🔲 | 🔲 🔲 🔲 🔲 | 🔲 🔲 ▾ 🔲 ▾ 🔲
<terminated> C:\Utilities\eclipse\workspace\Python\Learn to program\Script.py
Hello, world
Hello, world
Hello, world
Hello, world
Hello, world
The end
```

Figure 4.3: The bottom of the output showing that "The end" is printed out after the *while* loop output

4.2 FOR LOOPS

Another type of looping is a **for** loop. *For* loops are also used
to repeatedly execute multiple statements. The elements
that a *for* loop iterates through are more explicitly declared.
In the case of a *while* loop, the range was declared by stating
its least and greatest numbers (i.e. zero and 100). In the case of *for* loops,
the range is commonly declared through lists. Here is an example:

For

```
for i in [0,1,2,3,4,5]:
    print (i)
```

This code iterates through all the elements of the list and prints them out
one by one:

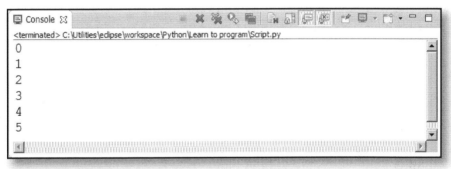

Figure 4.4: List elements printed out line by line.

Let's try to use the *for* loop for writing the sample code we wrote in the
while loop section:

```
for i in range(0,100):
    print (i)
```

Even though it looks like a list is missing in the previous code, this is
not completely true. The list is generated via the **range**
function. The *range* function here builds a list from zero to
100. Then the *print* function prints out every value of the
list. Again, numbers from zero to 99 would be printed out
line by line just as they were in the *while* loop example.

Range

Even though the results between the examples of the *while* loop and the example of the *for* loop are the same, you can see that the *for* loop has a different structure. *For* loops are primarily used when you want to iterate through lists, tuples or strings as in the following example:

```
for i in "Hello":
    print (i)
```

In this case of string iteration we would get this output:

Figure 4.5: Looping through string characters

Here is a more advanced example that integrates an *if* statement inside the *for* loop:

```
for key,i in enumerate("Hello"):
    if key % 2 == 0:
        print ("The letter {} is in an even
location ".format(i))
```

The output of this would be:

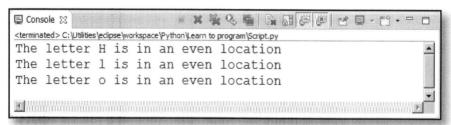

Figure 4.6: Printing out elements that have an even index inside the string

The variable *key* fetches the index of every string while the variable *i* fetches the strings itself. Both are variables. Notice that we also have a function called **enumerate** in the first line. This function makes possible the extraction of the indices and their assignment to variable *key*. Then, in the second line, the condition filters only the even index values fetched by variable *key*. Notice that

Enumerate

the way we filter the even numbers is by using an *if* statement. The "%" character here is a modulus operator that returns the remainder of a number. If the remainder of a number divided by two is zero, that number is an even number.

The third line under the *if* statement prints out some text written by us, together with the elements of the "Hello" string that have an even index value. Notice that the string elements are being printed using the *str. format()* utility which we have gone through before. The previous code is a good example of how different functionalities (i.e. *for* loop, *if* statement, and *str.format()* can be integrated together for more complex and useful programs.

Similarly to the previous example, you could try fetching the letters that have an odd index number. The only line you would have to change would be the *if* statement. This time we would go for a remainder of one, as that is what odd numbers yield:

```python
for key,i   in enumerate("Hello"):
    if key % 2 == 1:
        print ("The letter {} is in an even
location ".format(i))
```

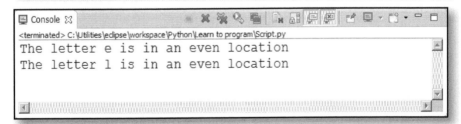

Figure 4.7: Printing out elements that have an odd index inside the string

Similarly as you looped through lists and strings, you would also do it with dictionaries but with some crucial differences that stand on the key-value structure of the dictionaries:

```
a = {"one":1,"two":2,"three":3}
for i in a:
    print (i, " corresponds to ", a[i])
```

In the first line, we declare the dictionary. Then in the second line we start the *for loop* block. The variable *i* will fetch the keys of the dictionaries. Remember that the *key* is the first element of a dictionary pair. Then in the third line we repeatedly print out the value of *i* that is the *key*. We also print out the phrase "corresponds to" and the *value* of the dictionary. Remember that a *value* is the second element of a dictionary pair. The output of this would be:

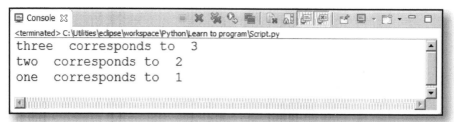

Figure 4.8: Printing out dictionary elements together with some text in between

As you can see, for loops and looping in general can be integrated into different scenarios where different types of data are encountered.

4.3 TRY, EXCEPT, FINALLY

Let's take a look at error handling in Python. As you master Python, you will stumble upon many errors which might be caused by different reasons. Many are syntax errors, meaning that they originate from typing mistakes made by the programmer. There are also other errors such as attribute errors, which are caused by inappropriate usage of commands. Here is an example of an attribute error raised by the program:

```
tuple = (1,2,3,4)
tuple.append(5)

for i in tuple:
    print (i)
```

In the previous code, we are trying to append an element to the tuple, but we know that tuples are immutable. Therefore, if you run the code, you will get an error:

```
Console
<terminated> C:\Utilities\eclipse\workspace\Python\Learn to program\Script.py
Traceback (most recent call last):
    File "C:\Utilities\eclipse\workspace\Python\Learn to program\Script
        tuple.append(5)
AttributeError: 'tuple' object has no attribute 'append'
```

Figure 4.9: Generated attribute error message

This error states that the object *tuple* has no attribute *append*.

> **Tip:** Strictly speaking, *append* is a **method** and not an **attribute**. However, to simplify error handling procedures, accessing a non-existent **method** or **attribute** is lumped under an **AttributeError** exception as shown in the text in red in Figure 4.9.

 These errors are encountered during execution and they are called **exceptions**. There is a way of handling *exceptions* and this is done through the **try and except** functionality.

Try and except provides a structure for handling and customizing error messages with the aim of more comprehensive error troubleshooting. Here is an example of *try and except*:

Try and Except

```python
tuple = (1,2,3,4)
try:
    tuple.append(5)
    for i in tuple:
        print (i)
except:
    print ("This is an error")
```

This code would give this result:

Figure 4.10: Customized error message

In the previous code, after the program reads the first line where a tuple is declared, it then executes the line under *try*. If the code of that line is correct and does not contain any errors, it will be normally executed and the line under *except* will be skipped. Otherwise, an exception will be raised and the program will execute only the line under *except* instead of the one under *try*.

There are different types of occurring errors. In the previous example you were introduced to an attribute error, which inside the Python language is known as an **AttributeError**.

An *AttributeError* occurs when the wrong attribute or method is tied to an object. In the previous example, the *append* method was tied to a *tuple*, but the *tuple* does not acknowledge it as its method.

There might also be different types of errors such as an **IOError**. An *IOError* is an error that occurs when the execution fails due to input or output errors such as "file not found" or "disk full".

As there are different types of errors that may occur, this gives the need to raise more than one possible exception. You will deal with more types of errors as you gain experience in Python. Here is an example where we handle an *AttributeError* and an *IOError*:

```python
tuple = (1,2,3,4,5)
try:
    tuple.append(5)
    for i in tuple:
        print(i)
except AttributeError as e:
    print('Error formed: ' , e)
except IOError as e:
    print('File not found:', e)
```

As appending elements to a tuple causes an attribute error, in the previous example, the line under the first exception will be executed and the result would be:

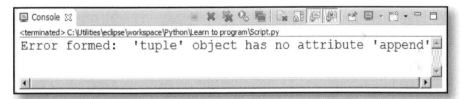

Figure 4.11: Customized error message followed by an attribute error

Notice that the second exception inside the previous code was ignored because the tuple appending error was not an *IOError*. The exception to be executed was the first one. This is because the first exception conducts an attribute error. Therefore, the execution of the first exception clause printed out the custom message "Error formed" and an internal error message embedded inside variable *e*. This error message is embedded inside variable *e* using the *as* command.

Besides *try and except*, there is also a **finally** clause. A *finally* clause is always executed before leaving the *try* statement, whether an exception has occurred or not. The clause is

Finally

written after the *except* statement:

```
tuple = (1,2,3,4,5)
try:
    tuple.append(5)
    for i in tuple:
        print(i)
except AttributeError as e:
    print('Error formed: ' , e)
except IOError as e:
    print('File not found:', e)
finally:
    print('The end')
```

In this case, the output of this code would be similar to the output of the previous code but with the "The end" phrase added in the end. Here is the output:

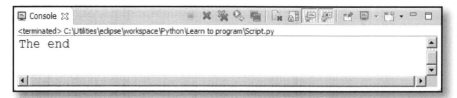

Figure 4.12: The output of the *finally* clause is added after the exception error message

These examples should give you a good start in handling different types of errors. Using this *try, except,* and *finally* syntax, you will be able to write more constructive and communicative code that can also be read and used by other users.

4.4 BREAK, CONTINUE, AND ELSE

The **break** statement is used to terminate a current loop and resume execution at the next statement. It can be used in both *for* and *while* loops. Here is an example of its use inside a *for* loop:

Break

```
list = [1,2,3,4,5,6,7,8,9]
for i in list:
    if i == 7:
        break
    else:
        print (i)
```

The output of this would be:

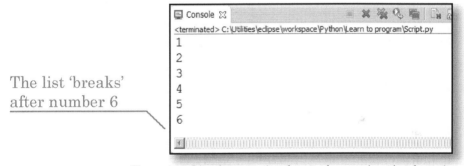

The list 'breaks' after number 6

Figure 4.13: List element printed up to element six as *break* sets it.

As you can see from the output, the printing out of the list elements ends at element six because we are telling the program to stop the execution when the *for* loop reaches the element seven. We do this using the *break* statement. In case there was no element seven in the list, the *else* statement would be executed.

A *break* statement can also be used in the same way inside a *while* loop. Here is an advanced example of its usage:

```
var = 10
while var > 0:
    print ("Current value :", var)
    var -= 1
```

```
if var == 5:
    break
```

> **Tip:** -= in the fourth line of the sample code above is the **Subtract and Assignment** operator. It will subtract 1 from the current value of **var** and then assign this new calculated value to **var**.

Notice that here we are using a decrementing *while* loop that starts at 10 and ends at zero. The loop block prints out some text together with the value of variable *var* for each iteration. Normally, the printing out would go from 10 down to zero and then stop if there was no *break* clause inside the loop, but in this case, this is not true. The *break* clause will terminate the printing out at element six. Here is the output:

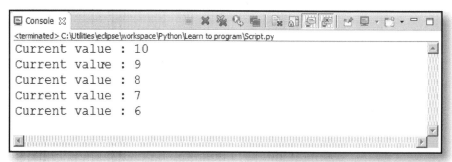

Figure 4.14: Numbers printed out from 10 down to six where the *break* clause terminates the loop

On the other hand, the **continue** statement is used to return the control to the beginning of the *while* loop. The *continue* statement rejects all the remaining statements in the current iteration of the loop and moves the control back to the top of the loop. Simply put, the *continue* statement continues the execution of the block. Here is the example:

Continue

```
list = [1,2,3,4,5,6,7,8,9]
for i in list:
    if i == 7:
        continue
    else:
        print (i)
else:
    print ("default ")
```

In this case we are telling the program to continue the expression even if the enumeration reaches the element seven. The output of the previous code would be:

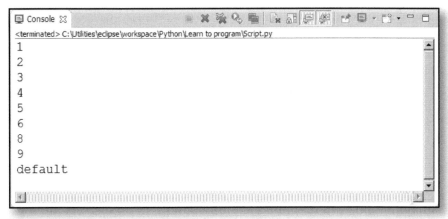

Figure 4.15: Elements printed out from the *for* loop block

The *else* statement itself has its own role inside a loop. When *else* is used inside a *for* loop, it is executed when the loop has exhausted iterating through the list. When *else* is used inside a *while* loop, the *else* statement is executed when the condition becomes false.

Both *break* and *continue* are useful functionalities that give more control to the work flow.

1. What would the following code do when executed?

```
a = 0
while a < 100:
    print (a)
    a += 2
```

    a. Print out numbers from zero to 100.
    b. Print out zero and two.
    c. Print out even numbers that fall between zero and 100.
    d. Display an error message.

2. What does the *range* functionality do?
    a. Generates a list.
    b. Defines the looping method.
    c. Generates a tuple.
    d. None of the above.

3. The *for* loop is commonly used to:
    a. Print out elements.
    b. Execute some code until a condition is met.
    c. Iterate through lists, tuples and strings.
    d. Iterate through integers.

4. What is true about *try* and *except*?
    a. The expression under *try* is executed when there is an exception.
    b. The expression under *except* is executed when the expression under *try* experiences an error.
    c. Neither of the expressions under *try* or *except* are executed when an *IOError* occurs.
    d. All above are false.

5. What happens when the condition above the *break* code line is not met?
    a. The *continue* part is executed.
    b. The line under *break* is not executed.
    c. The line under *break* is executed.
    d. The whole program breaks.

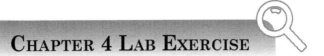

CHAPTER 4 LAB EXERCISE

You may have heard of the Fibonacci Sequence. It is a sequence of numbers where the next number is found by adding the previous two numbers together.

It follows this format:

$$Fn = Fn - 2 + Fn - 1$$

with initial values of $F0 = 0$ and $F1 = 1$

This sequence is truly something amazing, and is found throughout nature. By definition, the first two numbers in the Fibonacci sequence are 0 and 1, and each subsequent number is the sum of the previous two. There is also a geometrical representation of the sequence through a spiral. The area of each of the squares is equal to a number of the sequence.

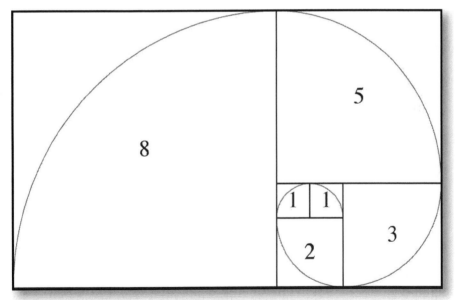

Figure 4.16: A Geometric representation of the Fibonacci sequence

Your task is to create a sequence of numbers for the Fibonacci sequence and stop at the first number that is greater than 100.

LAB SOLUTION

```
f0 = 0
f1 = 1
set = False
while True:
    fn = f0 + f1
    f0 = f1
    f1 = fn
    if (fn > 100):
        set = True
    else:
        set = False
    print(fn)
    if (set == True):
        break
```

The above code was input and executed in Eclipse as file fibonacci22.py. This is how the code and its output would look:

```
# Fibonacci2.py

f0 = 0
f1 = 1
flag2 = False
while True:
    fn = f0 + f1
    f0 = f1
    f1 = fn
    if (fn > 100):
        flag2 = True
    else:
        flag2 = False
    print(fn)
    if (flag2 == True):
        break
```

Console   PyUnit

<terminated> C:\Python2\ForWhile\Fibonacci22.py
```
1
2
3
5
8
13
21
34
55
89
144
```

Figure 4.17: Lab solution (upper part) and the generated Fibonacci Sequence output

Chapter 4 Summary

In this chapter you were introduced to the looping functionality. We discussed how looping comes to be very important due to its abilities to repeatedly execute multiple statements dependent on some conditions.

We explained both the *while* and the *for* loop. You should know that the *for* loop is specifically used when iterating through elements of lists, tuples, or strings. The while loop is more condition-oriented and less explicit in terms of the element it iterates.

We also went further and learned about error handling in Python in the sense of how to give better control to the encountered errors via the *try* and *except* functionality.

Furthermore, you were introduced to the *break* and *continue* tools that are used to better control the flow of the looping.

In the next chapter we will be talking about lists more in-depth. We will discuss list manipulation issues such as modifying, deleting, adding and sorting list elements and we will perform actions between different lists. You will get a better overall understanding of the usefulness of lists.

CHAPTER 5

LISTS

CHAPTER OBJECTIVES:

- You will deepen your knowledge of lists and their usefulness.
- You will learn how to modify lists by using the list-supported methods that add, modify or delete elements from a list.
- You will be introduced to the sorting functionality of the lists.

5.1 A CLOSER LOOK AT LISTS

We discussed *lists* in the second chapter of this book, and you should already know how to create one by now. However, given the high importance and usage of lists, we are now going to take a closer look at them.

You already learned how to access list elements using the indexing feature. Here is an example that reminds you how to do that:

```
a = ["a","b","c","d","e","f","g","h",
"i","j","k"]
print (a[2])
```

You would get the element "c" printed out because the index of "c" is "2":

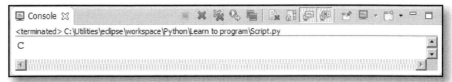

Figure 5.1: Element of list *a* with index "2"

Try to print out element "j" using its index. You will probably write this code:

```
a = ["a","b","c","d","e","f","g","h",
"i","j","k"]
print (a[9])
```

and get this result:

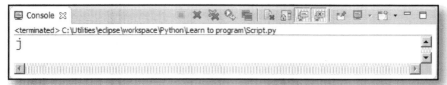

Figure 5.2: Element of list *a* with index "9"

This is correct, but not very efficient. You had to count the long way from left to right in order to get the index of element "j". Don't worry—there is a solution that is offered by negative indexing. Negative indexing starts by accessing list elements from right to left or from the last to the first, beginning at -1 and going backward. In our example, the "k" would be indexed with "-1", "j" with "-2", and so on. To print out the element "j" using negative indexing, we would write:

```
a = ["a","b","c","d","e","f","g","h",
"i","j","k"]
print (a[-2])
```

You will get:

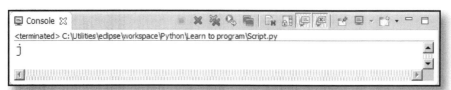

Figure 5.3: Element of list *a* with index "-2"

You got the same output as you did previously, but this time you didn't have to count the long way.

While working with lists and programming in general, you will probably come across tasks where you have to handle big lists. Counting their elements would be an exhaustive task. Therefore, knowing how many elements there are in a list can be very useful. The **len** built-in function will return the number of the elements that a list contains. *Len* stands for length. To find the length of list a, we would write:

Len

```
a = ["a","b","c","d","e","f","g","h",
"i","j","k"]
print (len(a))
```

The output would be:

Figure 5.4: The length (number of elements) of list *a*.

This means that the list has 11 elements. Here is a more practical example:

```
a = ["a","b","c","d","e","f","g","h",
"i","j","k"]
print (a[len(a)-1])
```

The output would be:

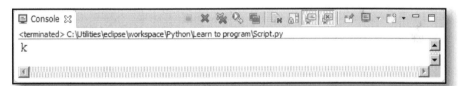

Figure 5.5: Element of list *a* with index "10"

As the length of the list is equal to 11, the "len(a)-1" will be equal to "10" which is the index representing element "k".

Besides accessing single elements from a list, you also learned how to access a range of elements:

```
a = ["a","b","c","d","e","f","g","h",
"i","j","k"]
print (a[3:8])
```

The output would be:

Figure 5.6: A range of elements of list *a* is printed out

You may want to print elements by iterating through indices with a step other than one, for example two:

```
a = ["a","b","c","d","e","f","g","h",
"i","j","k"]
print (a[3:8:2])
```

In this case, you are ignoring index four and six which correspond to elements "e" and "g". The output of this would be:

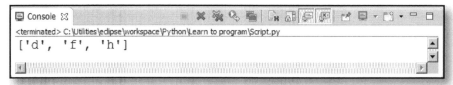

Figure 5.7: Elements of list *a* with index "3", "5" and "7"

Notice that elements "e" and "g" are missing in the output. This is because we defined a step of two, rather than one. In this case, the enumeration would start from index "3" but it would ignore index "4" by overstepping to "5".

> **Tip:** Please notice that a step of one when accessing a range of elements from a list does not have to be explicitly declared. A step of two or more has to be explicitly declared. A step of two might come in handy when you want to access only even or odd numbers from a list whose elements are numbers.

5.2 MODIFYING LISTS

Now we will go deeper into lists by learning how to modify them. With list modification we mean adding new elements, editing or deleting the existing ones. Each of these tasks is associated with a method or methods.

 A **method** is a function that belongs to an object and that does something to this object.

 Objects are data and a list is an example of an *object*. Here is an example of an *object* (list *a*) and a *method* (*append*) applied to the *object*:

```
a = ["a","b","c","d","e","f","g","h",
"i","j","k"]
a.append("l")
print (a)
```

The output from this would be:

Append

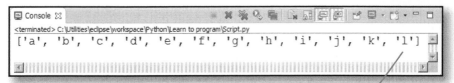

Figure 5.8: List with appended "l" element

Notice that a new element (l) has been added to the list. This was done through the *append* method.

Sometimes, you might want to not just add one element to a list, but an entire new list to a list- we can also refer to this as merging lists. This merging or extending can be done via the **extend()** method:

Extend

```
a = ["a","b","c","d","e"]
b = ["f","g","h","i","j"]
a.extend(b)
print (a)
```

The output of this would be:

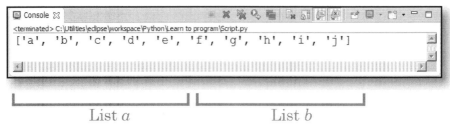

| List a | List b |

Figure 5.9: Merged list which is the extended list a.

You learned how to append an element to the end of the list and how to extend a list by appending another list to it. You might have asked yourself how one would add an element somewhere between the elements of the list. The answer is the **insert** method. The *insert* method adds an element to a specified position in the list.

Insert

Here is the example:

```
a = ["a","b","c","d","e"]
a.insert(3,"pause")
print(a)
```

You can see that the *insert* method takes two arguments ("3" and "pause"). The first argument defines the position index where the element is to be inserted while the second argument is the inserted element itself. The output of the previous code would be:

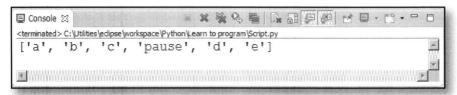

Figure 5.10: Inserted element in index "3"

As you can see, the element "pause" is the new element inserted in list a at index 3. The other elements beginning at index 3 have been pushed to the right. Sometimes, you might want to change the value of an element of your list. This is done easily, again by utilizing the indexing utility:

```
a = ["a","b","c","d","e"]
a[1]="x"
```

```
print(a)
```

The output would be:

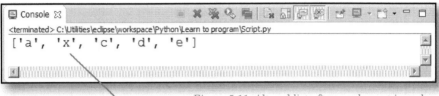

Figure 5.11: Altered list after an element is replaced

Notice that element "b" (having an index of "1") has been replaced by "x".

There might also be other scenarios when you are dealing with lists that contain numbers and you want to perform mathematical operations to the list elements. Again, you need to access them through indexing:

```
a = [10,20,30,40,50]
a[1] = a[1]*5
print(a)
```

In the previous code, we are changing element "20" by multiplying it by five.

The output is:

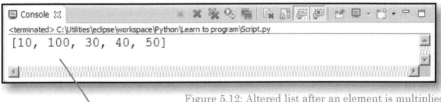

Figure 5.12: Altered list after an element is multiplied

Notice that the second value has changed to 100 which is the product of the multiplication of five and twenty.

As you might be expecting, there is also a way to delete list elements. A way to do this is through the **del** function. Here is an example of deleting an element from a list:

Del

```
a = [10,20,30,40,50]
del a[1]
print (a)
```

The output would be:

Figure 5.13: Altered list after an element has been deleted

If the deletion of only one element is not enough, we can also delete more than just one:

```
a = [10,20,30,40,50]
del a[1:4]
print (a)
```

In this case, the output would be:

Figure 5.14: Altered list after a range of elements has been deleted

The range *1:4* is the one that determines that the deleted items will be the one with index "1", "2", and "3".

While the *del* method deletes elements based on their index, it does not look at their value. If you were to delete an item whose index you don't know, instead of *del*, you would use the **remove** method:

```
a = [10,20,30,40,50]
a.remove(30)
print (a)
```

The output of this is:

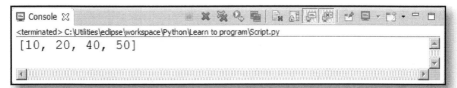

Figure 5.15: Altered list after an element has been removed

And lastly, another method that modifies lists – **reverse**.
Simply put, the *reverse* method reverses the elements of
the list:

Reverse

```
a = [10,20,30,40,50]
a.reverse()
print (a)
```

Here is the output:

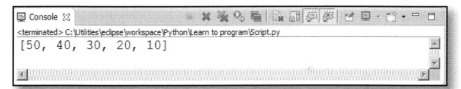

Figure 5.16: Reversed list after applying the *reverse()* function

All these methods are continuously used when working with lists. They
are commonly used in integration with looping, especially with *for*
loops. This combination makes the data manipulation and processing a
powerful tool of the programming language.

5.3 Sorting Lists

Sorting a list means rearranging the elements of the list according to a sorting criterion such as alphabetic or numeric. Like the other functionalities such as *reverse* or *remove, sorting* is also a method that is applied after a list. Here is an example of sorting list numbers from the least to the greatest:

```
a = [50, 30, 40, 20, 10]
a.sort()
print (a)
```

The resulted list from the sorting would be:

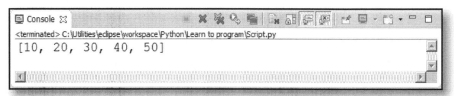

Figure 5.17: Sorted list from least to the greatest

You can see that list *a* has changed. Sometimes, you might want to retain your original list. In this case we would assign the sorted list to a new variable. This time we will use the *sorted()* method instead of *sort()*:

```
a = [50, 30, 40, 20, 10]
b = sorted(a)
print (b)
```

The output would be the same:

```
[10, 20, 30, 40, 50]
```

Figure 5.18: Sorted list from least to the greatest

Except this time the sorted list resulted from printing out list *b*.
You might have been thinking of a way to also sort the list from greatest
to the least. The *reverse* method, which we worked out in the previous
section, is the one that comes in handy:

```
a = [50, 30, 40, 20, 10]
b = sorted(a)
b.reverse()
print (b)
```

After the list has been sorted its default way (from the least to the
greatest) through the *sorted()* method, the order is then reversed through
reverse(). The output would be a reversed sorted list:

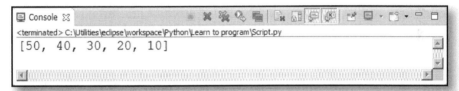

```
[50, 40, 30, 20, 10]
```

Figure 5.19: Sorted list from greatest to the least

You could also sort strings using the exact same methods. Here is an
example:

```
a = ["50", "30", "40", "20", "10"]
b = sorted(a)
print (b)
```

What you get from this is similar to the previous examples but this time
the elements are not numbers, but strings:

```
['10', '20', '30', '40', '50']
```

Figure 5.20: Alphabetically sorted list of string elements

Tip: Notice that even though the elements of the last list, based on our perception, look like numbers, for the program they are just strings. Everything inside quotes is a string and is therefore treated as a string. You cannot perform mathematical operations with strings, no matter if the characters are letters, symbols or numbers. Eventually, the elements will be sorted as strings.

Sorting can become very useful when storing data in lists. An example would be a list of people's names.

QUESTIONS FOR REVIEW

1. What is true about negative indexing?
   a. It provides an easy method to enumerate list elements starting from the end.
   b. It provides a method to consider positive numbers when working with lists.
   c. It only works with lists.
   d. It only works with number elements.

2. What would the code below do if executed?

```
if len(["a","b","c"]) == len(["abc"]):
        print (True)
else:
        print (False)
```

   a. Nothing.
   b. Print out True.
   c. Print out False.
   d. Print out the length of the lists.

3. How would you delete an element with index *a* from list *b*?
   a. b.remove("a")
   b. b.delete("a")
   c. del b[a]
   d. remove b("a")

4. Number *3* is missing from list *a = [1,2,4,5]* we need to add it again. There are different methods of adding number 3 to its proper position (after number 2) inside the list. Which of these methods would be an incorrect method of adding the number in its proper position?
   a. a.append(3)
      a.sort()
   b. a.insert(2,3)
   c. a.insert(-2,3)
   d. a.insert(3)
      a.sort()

CHAPTER 5 LAB EXERCISE

There is an algorithm called **Bubble Sort** that is used to sort a list of numeric values in ascending order. This algorithm compares two values at a time to see which value is larger. If the value on the left is larger, it will swap the two around. After looping through the process it will have ordered the numbers properly. This starts from the left and travels right. Once it reaches the end, it starts again. This process will be repeated until there is one complete pass through the set of numbers without any changes, which means that the numbers are in the right order, or until you have looped through $N - 1$ times, which is the maximum number of times needed. N is the number of elements provided in the set. The number list to rearrange is:

Bubble Sort

$$8 \ 7 \ 12 \ 4 \ 9 \ 6 \ 5$$

You will be dealing with nested loops here, so be careful with indenting. The proposed steps for the exercise are:

1. Creating the list with the elements in the order given previously.
2. Assigning the number of elements to a variable N.
3. Consider assigning a Boolean value to a variable.
4. Use the *while* loop for the rest of the exercise.

LAB SOLUTION

```
data = [8,7,12,4,9,6,5]
N = len(data)
swapped = True
while (swapped == True or N != 1):
    swapped = False
    position = 0

    while (position < N - 1):
        if (data[position] > data[position
+ 1]):
            temp = data[position]
            data[position] = data[position
+ 1]
            data[position + 1] = temp
            swapped = True
        position = position + 1
    N = N - 1

print(data)
```

This is how the solution and its output would look in Eclipse:

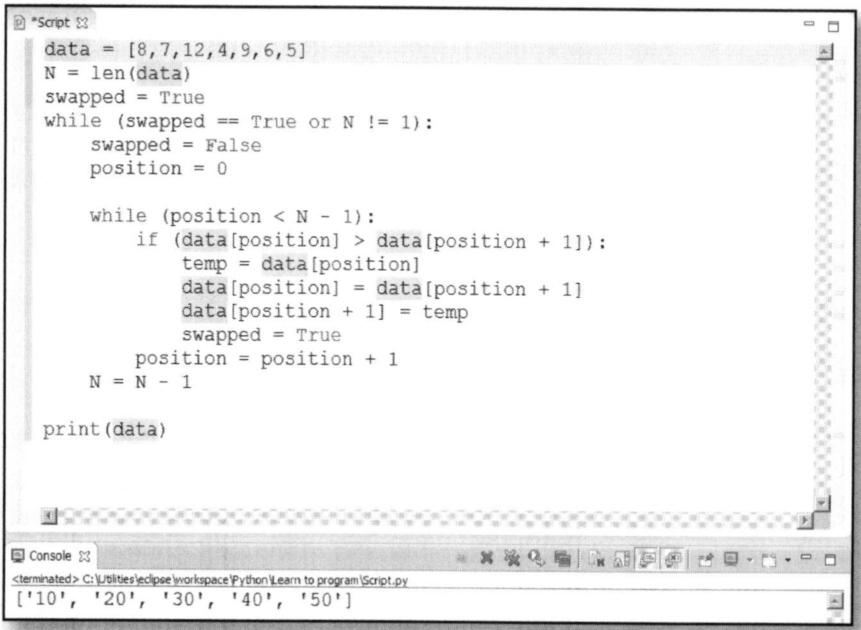

```
data = [8,7,12,4,9,6,5]
N = len(data)
swapped = True
while (swapped == True or N != 1):
    swapped = False
    position = 0

    while (position < N - 1):
        if (data[position] > data[position + 1]):
            temp = data[position]
            data[position] = data[position + 1]
            data[position + 1] = temp
            swapped = True
        position = position + 1
    N = N - 1

print(data)
```

```
Console ✕
<terminated> C:\Utilities\eclipse\workspace\Python\Learn to program\Script.py
['10', '20', '30', '40', '50']
```

Figure 5.21: Lab solution (upper part) script and the rearranged list (bottom part) after the script is run

CHAPTER SUMMARY

Even though you were already introduced to lists in the previous chapters, in this chapter you were able to expand your understanding of how to work with lists. You worked on accessing list elements using efficient methods such as negative indexing. Besides accessing single elements, we also discussed how to extract ranges of elements from a list.

You learned how to modify list elements by adding, deleting and editing them. To accomplish these modifying tasks, you were introduced to the *append, insert, remove,* and *del* methods. Furthermore, we discussed the *extend* method which is used to merge lists.

We also looked at the sorting aspect of the list elements. We went through the different approaches to sorting: the *sort(), sorted(),* and *reverse()* methods.

So far, you have encountered only static output that is read-only and does not allow its reader to perform any action. In chapter 6 you will be learning about user input, how to receive it and how to perform actions depending on it. You will see that input capability creates a sense of interaction between the end user and the program.

Python for Beginners

CHAPTER 6

RECEIVING INPUTS

CHAPTER OBJECTIVES:

- You will be introduced to the basic usage of the receiving input functionality.
- You will learn how to receive, use, and process user data input and give user-dependent output.

6.1 "PRESS ANY KEY TO CONTINUE"

In previous chapters you learned how to generate different output, but so far, the user that reads your output could not interact with the output other than to read it. In this chapter, you will be learning how to write programs that make the relationship between the user and the code output more interactive.

The proper tool here that allows the user to interact with the program is the **input()** method. The *input()* method keeps the program in a holding state, meaning that the execution is suspended at the *input()* line and can only be resumed by the user through certain actions. Here is an example:

input()

```
print('Hello!')
input('Press any key to continue')
print('Thank you')
```

As you can see here, the first line will print out some text, and then we prompt the user with a message ("Press any key to continue") via the second line. The text inside the *input()* parentheses is the message that will be displayed to the user. You can write anything you want inside those parentheses. After the message is displayed, program execution will be suspended and will only resume when the user presses a key. When the user presses a key, program execution will resume on the third line which will print out some text. The first execution of the code will give this output:

Figure 6.1: Output waiting for the user action

Notice that the third line was not executed because the *input()* method suspends program execution at the second line and waits for the user to resume by pressing a key on the keyboard. Besides pressing one or more keys, you should also hit the return key to signal to the program that you have finished pressing keys. After you press the return button, you should get this updated output:

Notice that a third line has been added to the output. This third line shows that the user has interacted with the program by allowing its full execution.

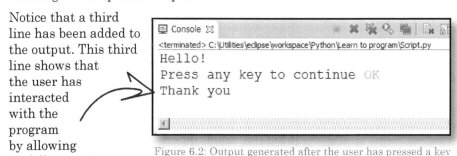

Figure 6.2: Output generated after the user has pressed a key

Tip: Notice that in the first example of this chapter we did not use double quotes (") but single ones ('). This is just a matter of style and there is no technical reason for choosing either way, as both of the quote types play the same role.

However, there is a scenario where you would have to use proper quotes. This is when your string contains quotes that have to be part of the string. If the string contains single quote characters, you would have to wrap it with double quotes and vice-versa.

An example of single quotes enclosed in double quotes:

"The boy cried 'Foul!' when he realized he had been cheated."

6.2 DATA INPUT

In the previous section we learned the basic usage of the *input()* method. The output we generated in the second example as shown in Figure 6.2 was very static in that no matter which key we pressed, the message to be displayed was always "Thank you". In this section we will learn a more interactive way to use the *input()* method.

Until now, you have assigned numbers and strings to variables in a very explicit way, such as:

```
a = 1
```

Besides this, there are also implicit assignments such as:

```
a = input("What is your name?")
```

Here, variable *a* will get a value depending on the text that the user types on the keyboard after the line is executed. To make the previous example more practical, we would add a *print()* command:

```
a = input("What is your name?")
print ("Hello" + a)
```

> **Tip:** Notice that the addition operator does not work only with numbers—it also works with strings, lists, tuples, and dictionaries. However, when used with data types other than numbers, the operator does not work as an addition operator but as a concatenator. In other words, it merges strings with strings, lists with lists, and so on.

Through the *print* function we are printing some text ("Hello") together with whatever the variable *a* contains.

When you first execute this block of code, you will be asked for your name:

Figure 6.3: Output waiting for the user to write a name

After you type in your name and press the return key, an updated output will be displayed, depending on what text you typed in.

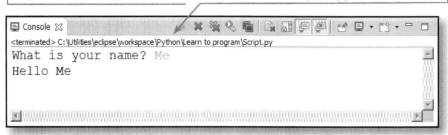

Figure 6.4: Output generated after the user has entered a name

By following these steps, you have been able to write a program that can communicate with the user. However, there is still more you can do.

Now, let's write a program that not only prints out the user input but also processes it before displaying. Here is the example:

```
a = input("Give me a number, I will give
you its half: ")
b = int(a)/2
print ("Half of " + a + " is " + str(b))
```

In the first line, we are assigning the user input to variable *a*. In the second line, we are calculating the half of the number that the user enters. Keep in mind that the input entered by the user is recognized and treated as a string by the program. If you want to use it as a number, you have to convert it to a number. This is exactly what we are doing in the second line. Using the *int()* function we are converting the user input to a number and assigning the converted value to variable *b*. Then in the third line, we use the *print()* function to print out three parts which are concatenated via the "+" operator.

Notice that in the third part (*str(b)*), we are again converting the value of *b*, which is a number, to a string. This is because we want to concatenate it with the first two parts which are strings. The output of this code after you have typed in a number (e.g. five) would be:

Figure 6.5: Output generated after the user has entered a number

As you progress with Python, you will come upon many use cases of the *input()* method and better understand its power in user interaction scenarios.

1. When running the following code:

```
list = [1,2,3]
a = input('Add a number to the list: ')
list.append(a)
print (list)
```

the user is prompted to type in a number. If the user types in "4", what would the program generate?

    a. 4
    b. [1, 2, 3, 4]
    c. [1, 2, 3]
    d. [1, 2, 3, '4']

2. When running the following code:

```
list = [1,2,3]
a = input('Add a number to the list: ')
list.append(int(a))
print (list)
```

the user is prompted to type in a number. If the user types in "4", what would the program generate?

    a. 4
    b. [1, 2, 3, 4]
    c. [1, 2, 3]
    d. [1, 2, 3, '4']

3. Which of the following is true?

    a. The two generated lists from question 1 and 2 were exactly the same.
    b. The generated list in question 1 contains only string elements.
    c. The generated list in question 2 contains only number elements.
    d. The generated list in question 2 contains mixed element types.

CHAPTER 6 LAB EXERCISE

In this exercise we will be using loops to check the user input. We want the user to input their gender. However, if it doesn't follow the correct format of being any of the possible replies below:

> m
> M
> f
> F

then we ask them to try again, and show the input option again. Once they have completed it successfully, after one or more iterations, we show a message telling them the gender they chose.

LAB SOLUTION

```
while True:
    gender = input('Gender: ')
    if(gender == 'M' or gender == 'm' or
gender == 'f' or gender == 'F'):
        break
    else :
        print('Please try again')

print('You are: ',gender)
```

This is how the code and the solution would look in Eclipse:

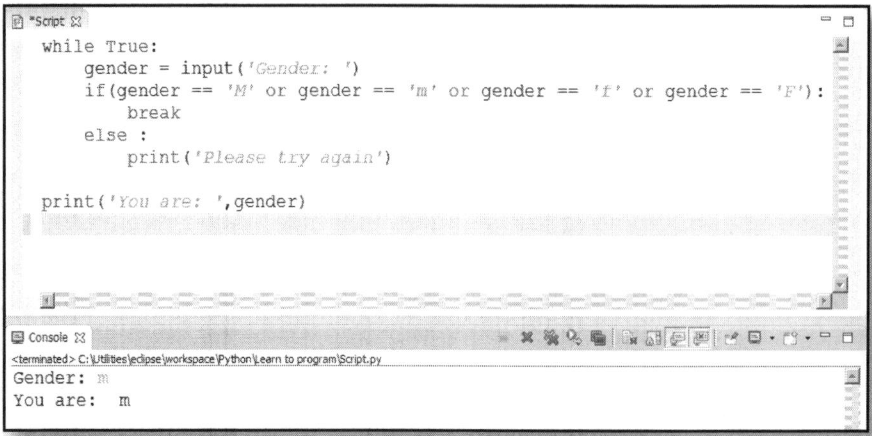

```
Script
    while True:
        gender = input('Gender: ')
        if(gender == 'M' or gender == 'm' or gender == 'f' or gender == 'F'):
            break
        else :
            print('Please try again')

    print('You are: ',gender)


Console
<terminated> C:\Utilities\eclipse\workspace\Python\Learn to program\Script.py
Gender: m
You are:  m
```

Figure 6.8: Lab solution code (upper part) and the generated output together with the user input (lower part)

CHAPTER SUMMARY

In this chapter you learned how to make your programs interact with the end user.
You were introduced to the receiving input functionality and you learned how to make the program execution dependent on the user action by using the *input()* function.

You expanded your understanding of the *input()* function by learning how to use the user input inside your program and how to manipulate it.

In the next chapter you will be learning ways of manipulating strings. These string manipulation procedures are referred to as string formatting in Python.

CHAPTER 7

PREDEFINED STRING FUNCTIONS

CHAPTER OBJECTIVES:

- You will learn how to use strings as objects by applying methods that alter them.
- You will learn how to access a full list of methods for every type of object in Python.
- You will learn to split string objects into parts and vice-versa.

7.1 USING STRINGS AS OBJECTS

Even though you already know what strings are, we haven't done many operations with strings. Strings are objects in Python and they are constructed by elements which are the characters that build them up. The string "Python" for example can be fragmented into six elements. This fragmentation nature of the strings makes them mutable. Most commonly, strings are modified using string methods, but there are also cases when string operators are used—an example of this is the "%s" operator, which is a placeholder that we have described in previous chapters.

In this chapter we are going to concentrate on methods that are applied to strings. However, before jumping into string methods, let's give a better illustration of the string fragmentation structure we mentioned previously. Here is a code example that accesses each element of a string:

```
for i in "This is a string":
    print (i)
```

The output of this code would look like this:

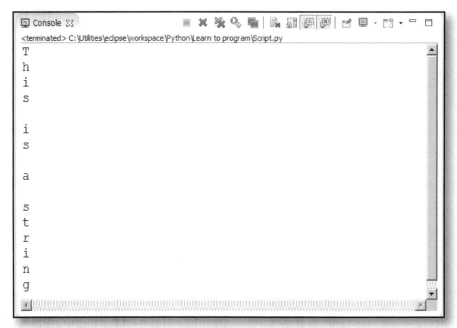

```
Console ☒                      ■ ✖ ✖ ✖ ✖ ■ | ■ ■ ■ ■ ■ | ■ ■ ▼ ■ ▼ □ □
<terminated> C:\Utilities\eclipse\workspace\Python\Learn to program\Script.py
T
h
i
s

i
s

a

s
t
r
i
n
g
```

Figure 7.1: String elements printed out one by one

As you can see, the string object has been divided into single objects that are its elements.

Here is a more complicated example that you have encountered when working with lists in the previous chapters:

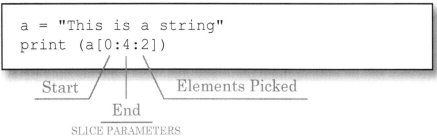

```
a = "This is a string"
print (a[0:4:2])
```

Start / | \ Elements Picked
End
SLICE PARAMETERS

Notice that we are using the same square bracket slicing syntax that we use with lists. In the first line, we are assigning a string value to variable a while in the second line we are printing a slice from the string. The first parameter inside the square brackets indicates the first element of the slice while the second indicates where the slicing ends. The third parameter is the step that the slicing uses to pick elements of the string.

Here is the output:

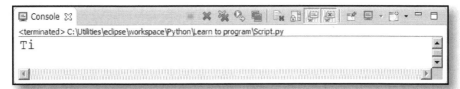

Figure 7.2: Output after the string has been sliced

To come up with this output, the code first picked the element with an index of zero from the string, which is the character "T". Then it stepped to the element with an index of two, which is the "i" character. Then it would step to index four, but the syntax 0:4 defines that the range stops at index four without including the element with index four. Therefore, the elements picked out from the strings were "T" and "i".

Let's have a look at methods used with strings—**string methods**.

Methods are functions that are applied to objects such as strings and that consequently alter or just use them for different processing purposes.

Suppose we need to count how many occurrences of an element there are in a string. There is a method that would come in handy in this case:

```
a = "This is a string"
c = a.count ("s")
print (c)
```

You may have already guessed the answer:

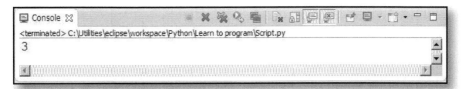

Figure 7.3: The number of "s" characters inside the string

Simply enough, we use the **count()** method to get the number of a certain character inside a string. In this case, we counted how many "s" characters our string contained.

count()

Tip: Be aware that string characters are case sensitive. If you counted for "S" instead of "s", the program would give an output of zero because "S" did not appear inside the text.

Here is another example of a method attached to a string object:

```
a = "this is a string"
c = a.capitalize()
print(c)
```

The **capitalize()** method is used to capitalize the first character of the string. Here is the output:

capitalize()

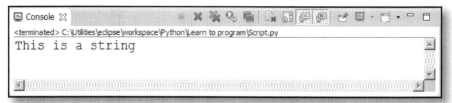

```
Console ✕
<terminated> C:\Utilities\eclipse\workspace\Python\Learn to program\Script.py
This is a string
```

Figure 7.4: The string after its first character has been capitalized

Tip: Some methods such as *capitalize()* work without having to take any parameter inside the parentheses. Some other methods such as *count()* would want at least one parameter given in order to work. There can also be other cases when certain methods will want exactly one, two or more parameters—this criteria always depends on the method.

Sometimes, we might want to capitalize all the first characters of the words contained inside the string. Here is a sample code that solves that:

```
a = "this is a string"
c = a.title()
print(c)
```

And here is the output:

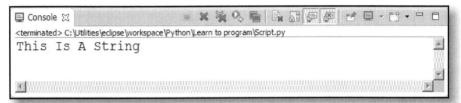

Figure 7.5: The string after the characters of every word have been capitalized

Tip: Objects such as strings may be associated with so many methods that it would be impossible to mention all of them here. You can get a full list of methods for a particular type of object, along with their definitions, while writing the code inside Eclipse. The method list is automatically displayed just after you have finished writing the instance name of the object and typed in the period, signaling that a method is about to be written. Figure 7.6 shows an example.

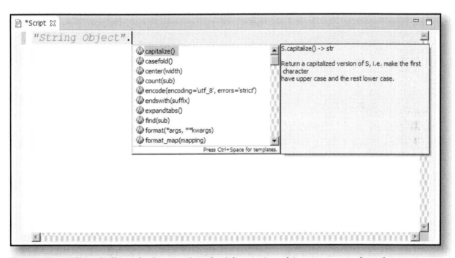

Figure 7.6: A list of all methods associated with a string object pops up after the programmer types in a period after the object instance name.

In the same way as described in Figure 7.6, you can access all the methods of every object.

7.2 SPLITTING AND JOINING STRINGS

While working with strings, you might come across issues where you have to organize, merge, or clean up certain text. As already mentioned, these tasks are part of the *string formatting* processes in Python. Splitting and joining strings are very important processes of string formatting. Simply enough, there are two methods that split and join strings, the **split()** method and the **join()** method, respectively.

split()

join()

Sometimes you might write programs that deal with file handling such as opening, modifying, or saving files that reside on your computer. This brings up issues with file names and paths. When there are too many files that need to be handled, looping in combination with string formatting functionality is used.

Let's take a look at a simple practical example of the string formatting application in file handling. Suppose we need to create directory paths using some initial information that we have inside a list:

```
foldersAndFiles = ["C:","Folder/Subfolder",
"picture.jpeg"]
```

As shown in the previous code, our list contains our computer drive name, our folder path, and the name of the file that we need to access. Suppose that the file *picture.jpeg* is contained inside the path generated by the folder names. We now need to generate a full correct path that can be used later to access the file. We need to get together all the list elements and join them with a slash character (/). Here is the code that would do that:

```
foldersAndFiles = ["C:","Folder/Subfolder",
"picture.jpeg"]
path = "/".join(foldersAndFiles)
print(path)
```

The output you get is a string:

Figure 7.7: Joined list elements using the *join()* method

This way, we have the whole path of the file named *picture.jpeg*. In the next chapters when we discuss file handling, you will understand that this path is used to access and process files that are identified with it.

Now, let's look at the *split()* method which does the opposite of *join()*. The *split()* method will separate the string at each occurrence of a given character.

Here is an example to illustrate what we are talking about:

```
print("This$text$contains$unwanted$symbols"
.split("$"))
```

Notice that the parameter that the *split()* method takes is the character we want to split the text at.

This is the output:

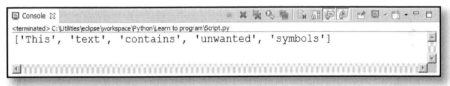

Figure 7.8: List generated by splitting a string using the *split()* method

Notice that the output of the *split()* method is a list that contains the split strings. If your intention was to clean up the text from the unwanted characters without having a list output, we could extend our code like this:

```
splitting =
"This$text$contains$unwanted$symbols".
split("$")
joining = " ".join(splitting)
print (joining)
```

In the previous code, we are first splitting the string by removing the "$" character from it and automatically converting the string to a list. Then we generate spaces between the words where the "$" was residing using the *join()* method and automatically convert the list to a string. Eventually you will get this output:

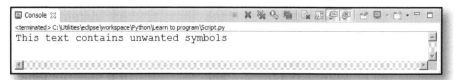

Figure 7.9: Text cleaned up after the *split()* and the *join()* methods have been applied to the string

Sometimes, you may want to split only a part of the string and leave the rest as it is. You can do this by using a second parameter inside the *split()* method:

```
print("This$text$contains$unwanted$symbols"
.split("$",2))
```

The second parameter indicates how many splits will be done starting from left to right. A parameter of two, as given in the previous code, would mean that only the first two occurrences will be split. This is what the output would look like:

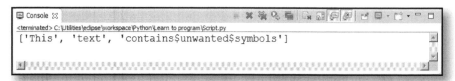

Figure 7.10: Generated list from a partly split string

The *split()* and the *join()* methods can be considered simple but very important string methods.

QUESTIONS FOR REVIEW

1. Which of the structures best represents the following code?

```
"String".title()
```

a. object.method()
b. method().object
c. object.title()
d. object.operator

2. What does the second line of the following code do?

```
a = "this is a string"
c = a.capitalize()
```

a. It changes the value of variable *a*.
b. It assigns the value of variable *a* to variable *c*.
c. It capitalizes the letter *a*.
d. It assigns the altered value of variable *a* to variable *c*.

3. What does the *split()* method return?
a. A split string.
b. Several strings.
c. A list.
d. A split tuple.

4. What does the *join()* method return?
a. A list.
b. A string.
c. Several joined strings.
d. A tuple.

CHAPTER 7 LAB EXERCISE

Within APIs (Application Programming Interface) you usually are provided with a username or id, and a secret key. Most of these are provided together with a separator such as a colon (:). Here is an example:

82914656273523:a4edFea2786DGex

You should separate these into two separate variables, and then we will do some validation on these. The format is id:key The id should always contain only digits (numbers 0-9) and always be 14 digits long. Besides digits, the key can also contain characters and can be any length over 10 characters and less than 20 characters. If all the credentials are okay, then just print out 'ID and Key are valid', if they aren't okay, display an appropriate message.

> **Hint**: Use the *isdigit()* method to check if the text contained inside a string object is a digit or not.

LAB SOLUTION

```
passed = '82914656273523:a4edFea2786DGex'

data = passed.split(':')

id = data[0]
key = data[1]
if(id.isdigit()):
    # Number is numeric.
    if(len(id) == 14):
        #Length of 14
        if(len(key) > 10 and len(key) <
20):
            print('ID and Key are valid')
        else:
            print('Key Length isn\'t
valid')
    else:
        print('ID wrong length')
else:
    print('ID isn\'t a digit')
```

The solution and the output would look like this in Eclipse:

```
passed = '82914656273523:a4edFea2786DGex'

data = passed.split(':')

id = data[0]
key = data[1]
if(id.isdigit()):
    # Number is numeric.
    if(len(id) == 14):
        #Length of 14
        if(len(key) > 10 and len(key) < 20):
            print('ID and Key are valid')
        else:
            print('Key Length isn\'t valid')
    else:
        print('ID wrong length')
else:
    print('ID isn\'t a digit')
```

Console ⊠

<terminated> C:\Utilities\eclipse\workspace\Python\Learn to program\Script.py
```
ID and Key are valid
```

Figure 7.11: Code that validates some text (upper part) and prints out the validation result (lower part)

CHAPTER SUMMARY

In this chapter you were introduced to strings as objects by learning how to apply methods that altered or extracted information from them.
You were introduced to some of the methods applied to strings such as *count()*, *capitalize()* and *title()*.

You learned how to look for a full list of methods inside the Eclipse platform, not only for string objects but for every type of object. You worked with the *join()* and *split()* methods and you should have an idea of their importance when working with tasks such as file handling.

In the next chapter you will learn how to write your own functions that return an output.

CHAPTER 8

CUSTOM FUNCTIONS

CHAPTER OBJECTIVES:

- You will be introduced to custom functions and their syntax.
- You will deepen your knowledge of custom functions by learning how to write more advanced functions containing more than one parameter.
- You will learn additional ways of using the returned output of the custom functions.

8.1 SYNTAX OVERVIEW

Throughout this book, we have gone through many functions used in Python, but so far, all these have been built-in functions that are predefined and cannot be customized by us. The *print()* function is an example of a built-in function. Its predefined role is to print out some text and we cannot change this behavior. The good news is that you can define your own functions using certain syntax.

Custom functions are blocks of code that may take some input, perform an action, and return some results accordingly. After a function has been written by the programmer, it can be reused in many situations inside the script.

Before going through examples, let's take a look at a model depicting the syntax used to write a custom function in Python:

```
def function_name(Parameter_1, Parameter_2,
Parameter_n):
    action
    return action_output
```

To begin defining a function, you will always have to use the **def** keyword. The keyword is followed by a custom function name and optional parameters. The first line of the block is closed with a colon (:). Then in the second line, you write the

def

actions you want to perform. These can be any type of actions such as mathematical operations, printing out text, manipulating objects, etc. The last line contains the **return** statement which passes the output that the function yields and also notes the end of the function. To illustrate the model, we are going to write a function that converts kilometers to miles using the convention that one kilometer is equal to 0.621371 miles:

return

```
def dist_convertor(km):
    miles = km * 0.621371
    return miles
```

 This is a function with one **parameter**. The *parameter* is the input value given to the function. It is given inside parentheses after the function name.

In this case we have only one parameter—the local variable *km*. In the second line we are declaring another local variable, *miles*. The second line is the action that the function performs, which in this case is multiplication. Then, in the third line, we are returning the value of the *miles* variable.

However, you may be disappointed when running this block of code because you would get no output out of it. This is because that code merely defines a function.

 To get the output we will need to **call** the function. *Calling* a function means executing it by inputting some values as parameters.

Here is how we *call* the function we defined in the previous code:

```
print(dist_convertor(10))
```

Tip: Be aware that in order to call a function inside a script, the function should reside in that script. In other words, the function block and the calling line should be in the same script file.

Here we are printing out the output of the function by putting in a parameter of 10, which are the number of kilometers we want to convert. The output will be the calculated miles.

This is how the whole code and output would look:

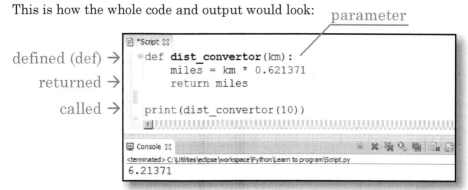

Figure 8.1: Defining, calling and returning the output of a custom function

The output value indicates that 10 kilometers is equal to 6.21371 miles. Once you define (write) the function, you can call it as many times as you want inside the same script using different parameters. Any time you call the function using different parameter values, the returned output will change accordingly.

8.2 MORE PARAMETERS

In the previous section we went through an example of a custom function with only one parameter. However, in the general model we explained in that section, you saw that we had multiple parameters. That means you and your needs determine how many parameters your function should have. You can also create functions that take no parameters:

```
def printing ():
    print ("This function simply prints out
some text")
printing ()
```

Here the function is defined in the first and the second line, while the third line is where we call it. In this case we don't need to call the function by using the *print()* built-in function because *print()* is contained inside the action of the function. Executing the previous code gives this output:

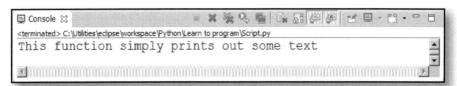

Figure 8.2: Output of a custom function that contains no parameters

Now, after having worked out a function with one parameter and another one with no parameter, let's have an example of a function with multiple parameters. Calculating the travel distance of a vehicle that moves at a certain velocity and acceleration at a given time would require a distance function with three parameters: velocity v, acceleration a, and time t. The formula that calculates the travel distance using these three variables is:

$$d = vt + (1/2)at^2$$

Tip: You can easily write the formula directly in Python without having to put it inside a function. However, you would have to do extra work every time you wanted to calculate it using different input values. Putting the formula inside a function has long-term benefits—it allows you to reuse that formula very easily by just calling the function.

Here is the function we would create to work out the distance formula:

```
def distance(v,a,t):
    d = v*t + 0.5*a*t**2
    return d
```

As you can see, we start the function using the *def* syntax and then we write a name for the function and the three parameters separated by commas inside the parentheses. The second line contains the formula, while the last line indicates the value the function will return after it has been called. So, let's call it by adding this line under the function:

```
print ("The travel distance is
",distance(30,5,20))
```

Tip: Notice that when calling a function that has multiple parameters, the order of the values of the parameters must be the same order you used when defining the function.

Here we are printing some text and the returned value of the function that corresponds with a velocity of 30, an acceleration of 10 and a time of 20. Here is the output you should get:

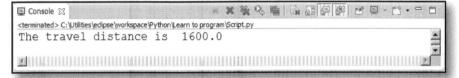

Figure 8.3: Printed text together with the returned value of the function

Notice that the returned value of the function is 1600.0. The function can also be utilized for further operations inside your code. Here is an example:

```
print(distance(30,5,20) - 600)
```

Running this line you will get:

Figure 8.4: The returned value after an operation with the function output

As you see, the function here acted as a variable by using its underlying value which is the value that the function returns as output. You will learn more about this in the next section.

> **Tip**: While dealing with functions, do not forget the variable scope issues that we discussed in previous chapters. You should remember that any variable that is defined inside a function is a local variable and cannot be used outside that function. Global variables are those variables that are defined outside a function and can be used both inside and outside functions.

8.3 MORE ON RETURNS

You might have noticed that in sections 8.1 and 8.2 we used two different ways to return the output for a function. Sometimes we used the *return* syntax and other times we directly used the *print()* function. There is a crucial difference between the two. Before explaining it, let's give an illustration through an example. First, let's use the return syntax to return an output of a function:

```
def triangle_area(base,height):
    return base*height/2

if triangle_area(10,3) >= 100:
    print ("Great triangle")
else:
    print ("Small triangle")
```

Here, we are first defining a function in the first two lines. Then, in the following lines we are using the returned value of the function inside a conditional block. In case the returned value of the function is greater than 100 area units, a message will be displayed. If the returned value of the function is less than 100 area units, another message will be displayed. In case you didn't notice, our function behaved just like a variable inside the conditional block. This is made possible by the use of the return syntax when defining the function.

Figure 8.5: Conditional output using the function returned value

You also know that if you want to print out the returned value of the function, you can just add a line at the bottom of the previous code, like so:

```
def triangle_area(base,height):
    return base*height/2
```

```
if triangle_area(10,3) >= 100:
    print ("Big triangle")
else:
    print ("Small triangle")
print (triangle_area(10,3))
```

And here is the output:

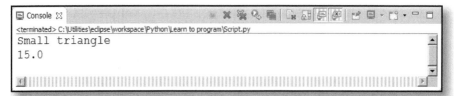

Figure 8.6: Conditional output using the function returned value also printed out on the second line

Now, try to write the same code as before but instead of using return, use the *print()* function as shown here.

```
def triangle_area(base,height):
    print (base*height/2)

if triangle_area(10,3) >= 100:
    print ("Big triangle")
else:
    print ("Small triangle")
```

The output you will get is this:

Figure 8.7: Program causing an error because the function output is not a number

This is because the function is just printing out the output as text, and not returning its actual value, which is a number. Using the *print()* function can be a quick way to merely print out the output, but when you want to use the output of the function in other operations as we did with the conditional block, the return value is the standard way to go.

QUESTIONS FOR REVIEW

1. Which of the following is a correct way of defining a custom function?
   a. def function():
      return
   b. function():
      return
   c. def function()
      return
   d. def function:
      return

2. What is not true about functions?
   a. Functions can be used as variables after they have been defined as far as the return syntax is used.
   b. Function parameters given when defining a function are variables.
   c. Function parameters given when calling a function are values.
   d. Functions cannot contain other functions inside them.

3. What is not true about variable scope and functions?
   a. Global variables cannot be used inside a function.
   b. Global variables can be used both inside and outside functions.
   c. Local variables cannot be used outside functions.
   d. Function parameters are local variables.

CHAPTER 8 LAB EXERCISE

In this lab exercise, your task is to create a function that will return a string that indicates the type of data that is passed to the function. The data types must be processed and checked as:

1. Alphanumeric
2. Digit only (this is number without decimal points)
3. Boolean

LAB SOLUTION

```
def checkDataType(string):
    myString = str(string)
    if(myString.isdigit()):
        return 'String is numeric'
    elif(myString.isalnum()) and not
myString=="True" and not myString=="False":
        return 'String is alphanumeric'
    elif(myString ==  "True" or myString ==
"False"):
        return 'String is Boolean'
    else:
        return 'unknown string type'

print(checkDataType("Sample"))
print(checkDataType(True))
print(checkDataType(960))
```

Notice that in the last line we are testing the function by calling it with a sample data type that is the string "Sample". This is how the code and its output would look in Eclipse:

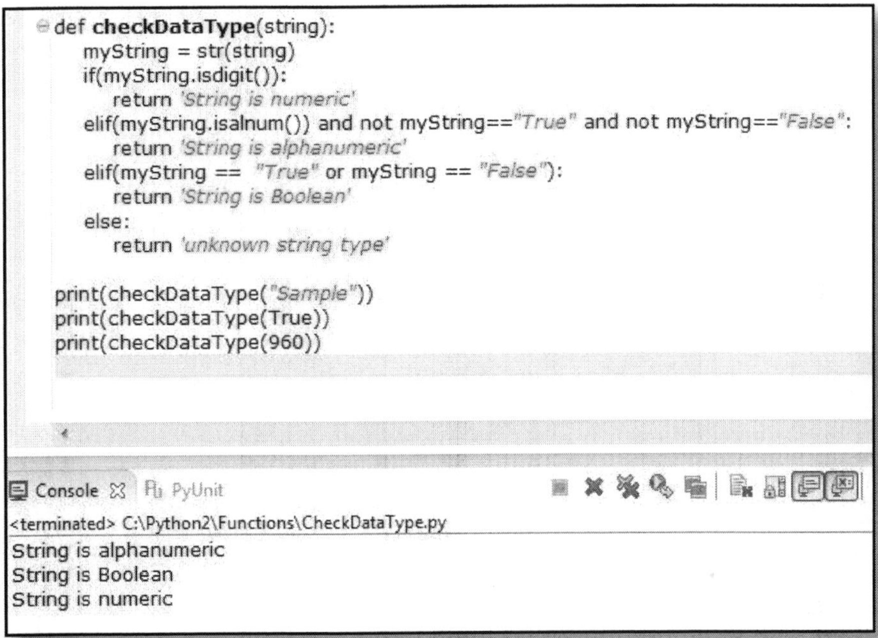

```python
def checkDataType(string):
    myString = str(string)
    if(myString.isdigit()):
        return 'String is numeric'
    elif(myString.isalnum()) and not myString=="True" and not myString=="False":
        return 'String is alphanumeric'
    elif(myString == "True" or myString == "False"):
        return 'String is Boolean'
    else:
        return 'unknown string type'

print(checkDataType("Sample"))
print(checkDataType(True))
print(checkDataType(960))
```

Console   PyUnit

<terminated> C:\Python2\Functions\CheckDataType.py

```
String is alphanumeric
String is Boolean
String is numeric
```

Figure 8.8: Lab solution (upper part) where the function is defined and called and the output (lower part)

CHAPTER SUMMARY

In this chapter you were introduced to custom functions and you learned how to define them. Going through examples, you practiced writing functions with a different number of parameters.

You also learned how to call functions you have already defined by inputting values as function parameters.

We discussed how functions can behave like variables and how their values are used for further operations inside your script. You should now know the difference between using the *return* and the *print* statements.

You were also reminded of the variable scope concept which is tightly related to the custom functions learned in this chapter.

In the next chapter, you will learn about classes, another critical functionality of every programming language.

CHAPTER 9

CLASSES

CHAPTER OBJECTIVES:

- You will be given an overview of classes and their related concept definitions.
- You will be introduced to a standard class sample and learn the syntax used to write a class.
- You will learn how to call an instance of a previously-defined class.
- You will be able to access and run methods that are contained within the classes you have created.
- You will be introduced to the class inheritance concept and you will also work with examples of inheritance between classes.

9.1 OVERVIEW OF CLASSES AND OBJECTS

 A **class** is a user-defined prototype or blueprint for an object. An object contains and defines a set of attributes that characterize it and other identical objects of its class. *Classes* are an easy and efficient way of storing identical code together.

After a *class* has been created, objects (also called instances) of it can be created and called. *Classes* come along with a set of concepts that you need to learn. Therefore, we will start by describing those concepts. At first, you might find it difficult to grasp all the details contained in the following list of definitions. However, you will slowly master them as you work with classes. Here are the definitions:

- **Class variable**
- **Data member**
- **Instance variable**
- **Inheritance**
- **Instantiation**
- **Method**
- **Object**

 A *class variable* is a variable defined inside a class of which a single copy exists, regardless of how many instances of the class will occur.

A *data member* is a class variable or an instance variable that holds data associated with a class and its objects.

An *instance variable* is a variable that is defined inside a class, for which each object of the class has a separate copy or instance.

Inheritance is a transfer of the characteristics of one class to another class that was derived from it. (For example, the class "dog" and "cat" would be derived or inherited from the class "animal" as they would have some methods (eat, sleep, etc.) that belong to the class "animal.")

An *instance* is an individual object of a certain class. *Instantiation* is the process that signals the creation of an individual object from its class.

A *method* is a function that is contained inside a class. Methods are run when a class instance or the method itself is called.

An *object* is a unique instance of a data structure that is defined by its class. An object is comprised of data members which are class variables and instance variables.

QUESTIONS FOR REVIEW

1. Which of the following best describes a class?
   a. A structure of categories and sub-categories used to store data.
   b. A prototype dictionary used to store and return data passed to it.
   c. A function that uses *self* as a parameter.
   d. A prototype with methods within it.

2. What is a class method?
   a. A method to return output generated from the class.
   b. A function.
   c. A built-in object.
   d. An inherited function from an existing class.

9.2 USING "CLASS"

After having defined the concepts that are related to classes, let's now create our first class. We are going to write a class called "Person". From our life experience, we know that a person has some attributes such as gender, name etc. These attributes will be the variables that are going to be passed to the class we will create. Here is the code block to create your first class:

```
class Person:
def __init__(self,gender,name):
self.Gender = gender
self.Name = name
def display(self):
print("You're a ",self.Gender,", and your
name is ", self.Name)
```

Notice that this code is just the class creation part. As with functions, you will not get any output if you run this code. You need to call an instance of the class to get some results. Calling a class instance would be to run the class by passing some attribute values to it. Before we do that, let's first go through the code and explain it.

We intentionally used the term "class" in the title of this section. Just like the *def* keyword which we used to start writing a function, the *class* keyword is used to start writing a class. This is what we do in the first line of the code. Here, we decided to name this class "Person".

The second line of the code block is also a routine when defining a class. It is where the class is initialized through the **__init__** method and where the class attributes are given. The *self* attribute is obligatory and it is always given to the class. The other two attributes, gender and name, are given by us.

init

Tip: Even though the *self* parameter is given any time a class is defined, it is not a keyword in Python—you can use any name for it. However, *self* is a strong convention among programmers and we suggest you use the same word.

In the third and fourth lines of the previous code block we are connecting all the attributes to *self*. In these lines, *self* is an object and *Gender* and *Name* are variables within that object. We are capitalizing Gender and Name here to make it visible that they are actually not the attributes we passed to the __init__ method. Instead, they are local variables.

Then in the fifth and sixth lines, we define a custom method and call it "display". We pass *self* to this method. Because *self* now contains all the attributes of the class, we can use them within the method. In this case, we are printing out some text along with the attributes that will be given to the class when being called.

To get an understanding of what this class does, we need to call an instance of it. To do that, you need to add the following line under the class you created:

```
Person("male","Me").display()
```

As you see here, you are calling an instance of the class using "male" as *gender* and "Me" as *name*. In this case we are running the *display* method contained within the class. Here is the output you will get:

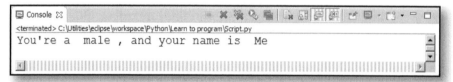

Figure 9.1: Displayed text from the *display* method after the custom class has been called

Notice the syntax used to call the class. First, we wrote the class name and two attribute instances inside the parentheses. Then, we called one of the methods defined inside the class, which in this case is the function *display()* which prints out some text along with the attributes of the class.

QUESTIONS FOR REVIEW

1. How do you start writing a class?
   a. class classname:
   b. class __init__
   c. def class:
   d. def class():

2. What would you do to get an output from a defined class?
   a. Return a value within the class functions.
   b. Call a class instance.
   c. Print out the class.
   d. Print out the class functions.

LAB ACTIVITY

Consider the previous class example:

```
class Person:
def __init__(self,gender,name):
self.Gender = gender
self.Name = name
def display(self):
print("You're a ",self.Gender,", and your
name is ", self.Name)
```

Add another attribute to this class such as "age", incorporate it inside the display() method, and call an instance of the class.

LAB SOLUTION

```python
class Person:
    def __init__(self,gender,name,age):
        self.Gender = gender
        self.Name = name
        self.Age = age
    def display(self):
        print("You're a ",self.
Gender,", your name is ", self.Name, ", and
you are ", self.Age," year old")

Person("male","Me",25).display()
```

Here is how the solution and the output look in Eclipse:

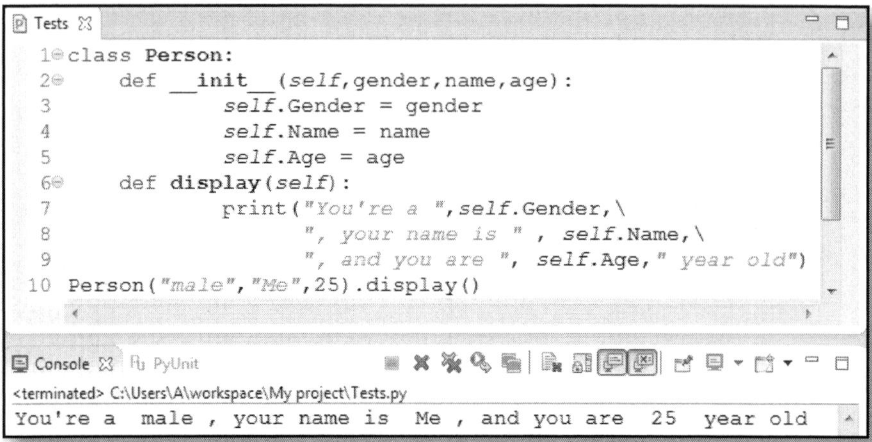

```
 1  class Person:
 2      def __init__(self,gender,name,age):
 3          self.Gender = gender
 4          self.Name = name
 5          self.Age = age
 6      def display(self):
 7          print("You're a ",self.Gender,\
 8              ", your name is " , self.Name,\
 9              ", and you are ", self.Age," year old")
10  Person("male","Me",25).display()
```

```
Console ⊠  PyUnit
<terminated> C:\Users\A\workspace\My project\Tests.py
You're a  male , your name is  Me , and you are  25  year old
```

Figure 9.2: A class with three attributes and an instance of it.

9.3 USING METHODS

As you've learned in section 9.1, a method is a function that is contained inside a class. However, methods are not exactly functions. Let's look at this example:

```
class Person:
def __init__(self,gender,name):
self.Gender = gender
self.Name = name

def display(self):
print("You're a ",self.Gender,", and your
name is ", self.Name)
```

What we have here is a class that has two methods. The first is the built-in *__init__* method which is used to initialize the class. More specifically, we can refer to *__init__* as a constructor when an instance of the class is created. The second method of our "Person" class is the *display* method which we created for printing out some text.

Once the class and its methods have been created, you can access them using the *object.method()* syntax:

```
Person("male","Me").display()
```

In this example, the part before the period is the object, and the part after that is the method. The period itself is used after the object to indicate that a method of the object is to be applied.

Notice that when we defined the *display* method, we used some variables such as *self.Gender* and *self.Name* within the body of the method. However, these two variables were not included as parameters of the *display* method. The key here is the use of the *self* variable and the *__init__* method. Using the *__init__* method you can define all the variables you want to use within the methods of a class.

Though, you are not restricted to adding new variables to the methods you define after the *__init__* method. Here is an example where we add another variable to the *display* method:

```
class Person:
    def __init__(self,gender,name):
        self.Gender = gender
        self.Name = name

    def display(self,lastName):
        print("You're a ",self.Gender,",
and your name is ", self.Name, lastName)
```

Notice that this time we are inputting a parameter to the display method. To call an instance of this class, we would have to add the following line under the previous code:

```
Person("male","Me").display("Pyto")
```

Here is how this example would look in Eclipse:

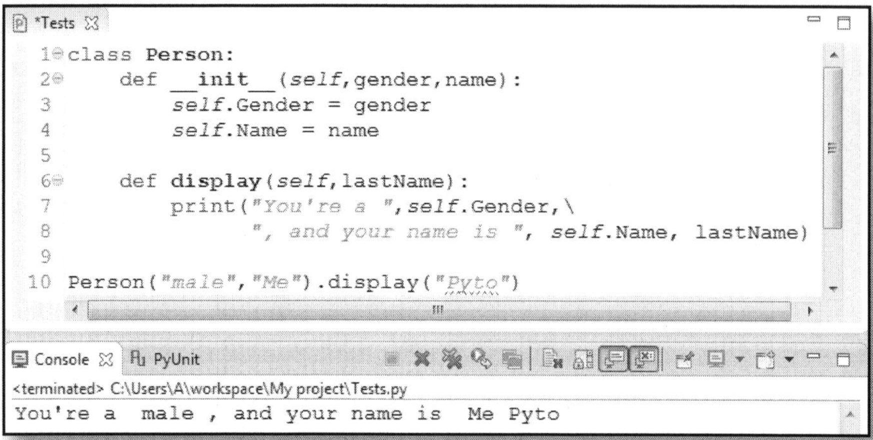

Figure 9.3: Defining a class and running an instance of it.

Try experimenting! Input your own variable instances such as name, gender and last name to see how your output changes. Once a class has been defined, class instances can also be assigned to global variables. Here is the example:

```
class Person:
    def __init__(self,gender,name):
        self.Gender = gender
        self.Name = name

    def display(self,lastName):
        print("You're a",self.Gender, "and
your name is",self.Name, lastName)

Person1=Person("male","Me")
Person2=Person("female","Anne")
Person3=Person("female","Frida")

Person1.display("Pyto")
Person2.display("Pyto")
Person3.display("Pyto")
```

Here is how the last example would look in Eclipse:

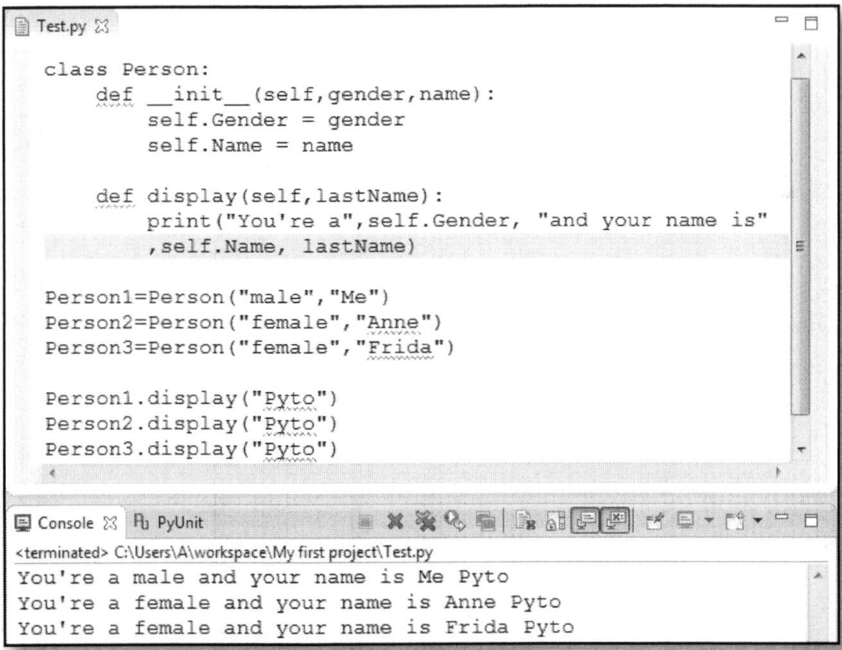

Figure 9.4: Defining a class: assigning class instances to global variables and running the class associated methods.

This way, we can call the same method, but with different variables by getting different outputs. In programming, this is called **encapsulation**.

1. Which of the following is not a keyword in Python?
   a. self
   b. def
   c. class
   d. __init__

2. What is the correct method of calling a class instance method?
   a. class().method()
   b. class.method
   c. class().method
   d. class.method()

LAB ACTIVITY

Modify the previous example:

```
class Person:
    def __init__(self,gender,name):
        self.Gender = gender
        self.Name = name

    def display(self,lastName):
        print("You're a ",self.Gender,",
and your name is ", self.Name, lastName)
```

By including all the three attributes (i.e. gender, name, and lastName) inside the __init__ method, we leave the display() method with only the self default attribute. We then call an instance of the class. The output has to be identical to the output of the original code.

Lab Solution

```
class Person:
    def __init__
(self,gender,name,lastName):
        self.Gender = gender
        self.Name = name
        self.lastName = lastName
    def display(self):
        print("You're a ",self.Gender,\
            ", and your name is ", self.
Name, self.lastName)
Person("male","Me","Pyto").display()
```

This is how the solution and the output would look in Eclipse:

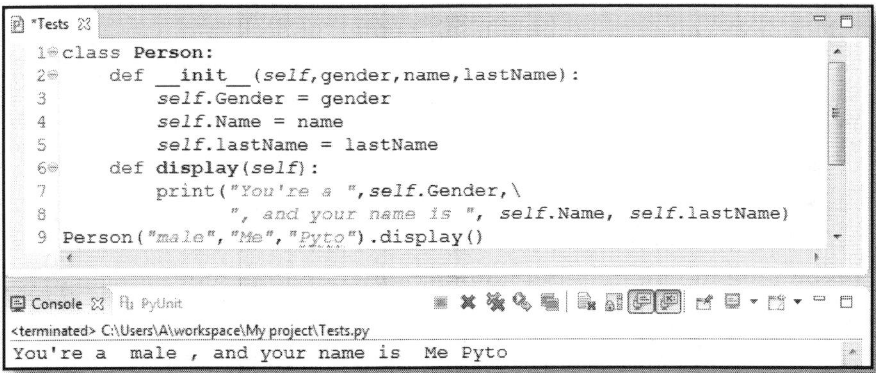

```
1 class Person:
2     def __init__(self,gender,name,lastName):
3         self.Gender = gender
4         self.Name = name
5         self.lastName = lastName
6     def display(self):
7         print("You're a ",self.Gender,\
8             ", and your name is ", self.Name, self.lastName)
9 Person("male","Me","Pyto").display()
```

```
Console ⊠  PyUnit
<terminated> C:\Users\A\workspace\My project\Tests.py
You're a  male , and your name is  Me Pyto
```

Figure 9.5: Class "Person" having all the attributes inside the *__init__* method.

9.4 USING OBJECT DATA

In the previous sections of this chapter you were introduced to an example of a class. Even though we can have several class instances, the data is stored within the objects and not the class. We worked with some variables which we fetched using the *display* method. Here we are going to have a similar example, but this time we are going to have some scalability in our code. Let's start writing our class example little by little. Here is how we start writing the class which, as you already know, is by defining the *__init__* method:

```
class Example:
def __init__(self, **kwargs):
self.variables = kwargs
```

In the very first line, we define the name of our class, which is "Example". The *__init__* method consists of the single third line which initializes the class. Here is also where we write the variables. We have the *self* default variable and another variable called **kwargs*.
Like *self*, **kwargs* is also not just a user-defined variable. In Python, *kwargs* is referred to as a **keyword argument**. Any parameter that you pass to the *__init__* method will be stored in a dictionary named *kwargs*. If there is only one asterisk placed before *kwargs* (such as **kwargs*) the parameters would be passed in the form of a tuple. In the last line of the code, we are assigning the dictionary to a variable inside our class. There is no need to use asterisks in this assignment statement.

Keyword Argument

Let's write the next part of the class. Paying attention to the indentation aspect, you will have to add these lines under the previous code:

```
def set_vars(self,k,v):
    self.variables[k] = v
```

Here we are creating another method which we have named *set_vars*. This method will populate the *kwargs* dictionary with keys and values. In this case, the *k* variable will hold the keys and *v* will hold the values. In the first line, the parameters (*self, k* and *v*) of the *set_vars* method are defined. The second line should be familiar to you. It is where the dictionary is being populated with keys and values. In this case, *self*.

variables is the variable that contains the dictionary *kwargs*.

Now, let's define a method that gets and returns the data that has already been stored in the dictionary. You will have to add this block of code under the previous one:

```
def get_vars(self,k):
    return self.variables.get(k, None)
```

This method will return the data of the dictionary based on the key we pass in. In the first line, we start defining the method and pass the *self* and *k* variables as arguments.

 Then, in the second line we use the predefined function **get** which is a dictionary method used to return dictionary values based on their corresponding key.

When we call this method later, using a key instance that does exist inside the dictionary, we will get the corresponding value; otherwise, if the key instance is not contained within the dictionary, we will get "None".

Putting all the previous parts together wraps up the creation of the class *Example:*

```
class Example:
    def __init__(self, **kwargs):
        self.variables = kwargs
    def set_vars(self,k,v):
        self.variables[k] = v
    def get_vars(self,k):
        return self.variables.get(k, None)
```

Now we can call some class instances. To do that, you need to add other lines of code under the class you defined and showed previously:

```
var = Example(age=25, location='AL')
var.set_vars('name','Me')
print(var.get_vars('name'))
print(var.get_vars('age'))
```

In the first line here, we are assigning an instance of the class to variable *var*. This class instance is passed with two parameters that are the two key-value pairs that will populate the dictionary.

Then, in the second line we populate the dictionary with one more pair of key and value. At this point, the dictionary within the class has three pairs.

In the last two lines of code, we are calling the *get_vars()* method which returns the corresponding value of a given key. In the first case, the given key is "name" and in the second one the key is "age". If these keys are within the dictionary of our class, their corresponding values will be displayed, otherwise *None* will be printed out.

The following figure gives the big picture of the whole example that we used throughout this section:

```
Test.py ⊠
    class Example:
        def __init__(self, **kwargs):
            self.variables = kwargs
        def set_vars(self, k, v):
            self.variables[k] = v
        def get_vars(self, k):
            return self.variables.get(k, None)
    var = Example(age=35, Location='US')
    var.set_vars('name', 'Me')
    print(var.get_vars('name'))
    print(var.get_vars('age'))


Console ⊠   PyUnit
<terminated> C:\Users\A\workspace\My first project\Test.py
Me
35
```

Figure 9.6: Defining a class that fetches the values of the keys from a dictionary.

This is how you use the data stored inside an object created and stored inside a custom class. This class can be used inside the program whenever you need it.

QUESTIONS FOR REVIEW

1. What would "*kwargs" indicate when passed as a parameter of a class?
    a. Method parameters will be stored in a dictionary called "kwargs".
    b. Method parameters will be stored in a tuple called "kwargs".
    c. Method parameters will be stored in a list called "kwargs".
    d. Method parameters will be stored in a keyword argument database.

2. In the previous example, what does the *get_vars*() method do?
    a. It gets the variables of the class.
    b. It returns the age of the user.
    c. It returns the corresponding value of a dictionary key.
    d. It returns the corresponding key of a dictionary value.

LAB ACTIVITY

Modify the previous code example:

```python
class Example:
    def __init__(self, **kwargs):
        self.variables = kwargs
    def set_vars(self,k,v):
        self.variables[k] = v
    def get_vars(self,k):
        return self.variables.get(k, None)

var = Example(age=25, location='AL')
var.set_vars('name','Me')
print(var.get_vars('name'))
print(var.get_vars('age'))
```

so that you get this output:

Figure 9.7: The expected output after the original code has been modified.

LAB SOLUTION

```python
class Example:
    def __init__(self, **kwargs):
        self.variables = kwargs
    def set_vars(self,k,v):
        self.variables[k] = v
    def get_vars(self,k):
        return self.variables.get(k, None)

var = Example(age=25, location='AL')
var.set_vars('name','Me')
print(var.get_vars('Name'))
print(var.get_vars('Age'))
```

Note: As you can see, one solution would be to simply look for two keys that do not exist in the dictionary such as "Name" and "Age". We populated our dictionary with the keys "age" and "name" and because strings are case-sensitive in Python, the program could not match the given keys "Name" and "Age" with the ones that the dictionary contained.

Here is the solution and the output as shown in Eclipse:

```
 Tests ⌧                                                    ▭

 1  class Example:
 2      def __init__(self, **kwargs):
 3          self.variables = kwargs
 4      def set_vars(self,k,v):
 5          self.variables[k] = v
 6      def get_vars(self,k):
 7          return self.variables.get(k, None)
 8
 9  var = Example(age=25, location='AL')
10  var.set_vars('name', 'Me')
11  print(var.get_vars('Name'))
12  print(var.get_vars('Age'))

 Console ⌧  Hu PyUnit      ■ ✗ ⁊ ⚖ 🗐 | 🗟 🔊 📧📧 🛱 🗐 ▾ 📂 ▾  ▭
 <terminated> C:\Users\A\workspace\My project\Tests.py
 None
 None
```

Figure 9.8: Class that fetches values from a dictionary and an instance of it returning no matched keys.

9.5 INHERITANCE

As we already defined, *inheritance* is a transfer of the attributes of a class to another class that was derived from it. *Inheritance* makes it possible to use the methods of a class within another class. This way, you don't have to define the same methods again in another class when writing large programs. To illustrate inheritance, we are going to use two different classes: the "animals" class and the "dogs" class. Animals share some similar actions such as eating, breathing, and sleeping. A dog is part of the animal kingdom and performs the same actions that an animal does. Therefore, the "dogs" class can inherit the actions from the "animals" class. The class that the methods are inherited from is called a **superclass**. In our example, the *superclass* will be "animals". Let's write the *superclass*:

Superclass

```
class animals:
    def eat(self):
        print ("I can eat.")
    def breath(self):
        print ("I can breathe.")
    def sleep(self):
        print ("I can sleep.")
```

What we have here is a class with three simple methods that simply print out some text. Now we want to create another class that summarizes what a dog can do. Instead of rewriting the list of actions that animals perform, we can just inherit them:

```
class dogs(animals):
    def bark(self):
        print("I can bark.")
    def guard(self):
        print("I can guard.")
```

The first line of the code block is where the class "dog" is declared to be inherited from the class "animals". This means that the class "dog" has now all the same methods that the class "animals" has. This is simply done by putting the superclass "animals" inside the parentheses. The next lines are other normal methods that are appropriate for the "dogs" class. These methods are contained only by the class "dog". Try to add the following lines to see the output:

```
animals().eat()
dogs().sleep()
```

Notice that even though the *sleep* method was not explicitly defined inside the "dogs" class, it is a method of that class. Here is what the complete code example would look like in Eclipse:

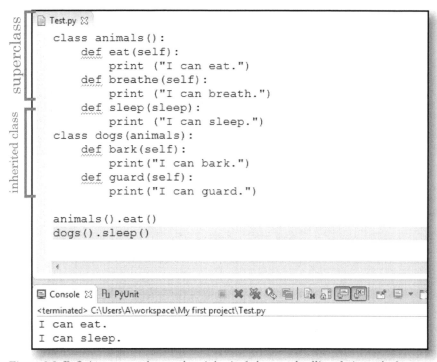

Figure 9.9: Defining a superclass and an inherited class, and calling their methods.

> **Tip:** It is possible that in the inherited class you might define a method that was already defined in the superclass. In this case, the new method in the inherited class will supersede the method in the superclass meaning that the new method is the one that will be executed when the class is called.

QUESTIONS FOR REVIEW

1. When would you use inheritance?
   a. When you want to use the parameters of a function in another function.
   b. When working with identical classes.
   c. When a class you want to create is a "subset" of another class.
   d. When some of the methods of a class you want to create are contained in an existing class.

2. How would you start writing the class *child* that is inherited from the class *parent*?
   a. class child():
   b. class child.parent()
   c. class child:
      extend parent;
   d. class child(parent)

LAB ACTIVITY

Add another class called "hound" to the previous code example:

```python
class animals:
    def eat(self):
        print ("I can eat.")
    def breath(self):
        print ("I can breathe.")
    def sleep(self):
        print ("I can sleep.")
class dogs(animals):
    def bark(self):
        print("I can bark.")
    def guard(self):
        print ("I can guard.")

animals().eat()
dogs().sleep()
```

The "hound" class will represent the hound type of dog which can perform all the actions that an animal and a dog can. In addition, a hound can also hunt.

```
class animals:
    def eat(self):
        print ("I can eat.")
    def breath(self):
        print ("I can breathe.")
    def sleep(self):
        print ("I can sleep.")
class dogs(animals):
    def bark(self):
        print("I can bark.")
    def guard(self):
        print("I can guard.")
class hound(dogs):
    def hunt(self):
        print ("I can hunt")

animals().eat()
dogs().sleep()
hound().hunt()
```

This is how the solution and its output look in Eclipse:

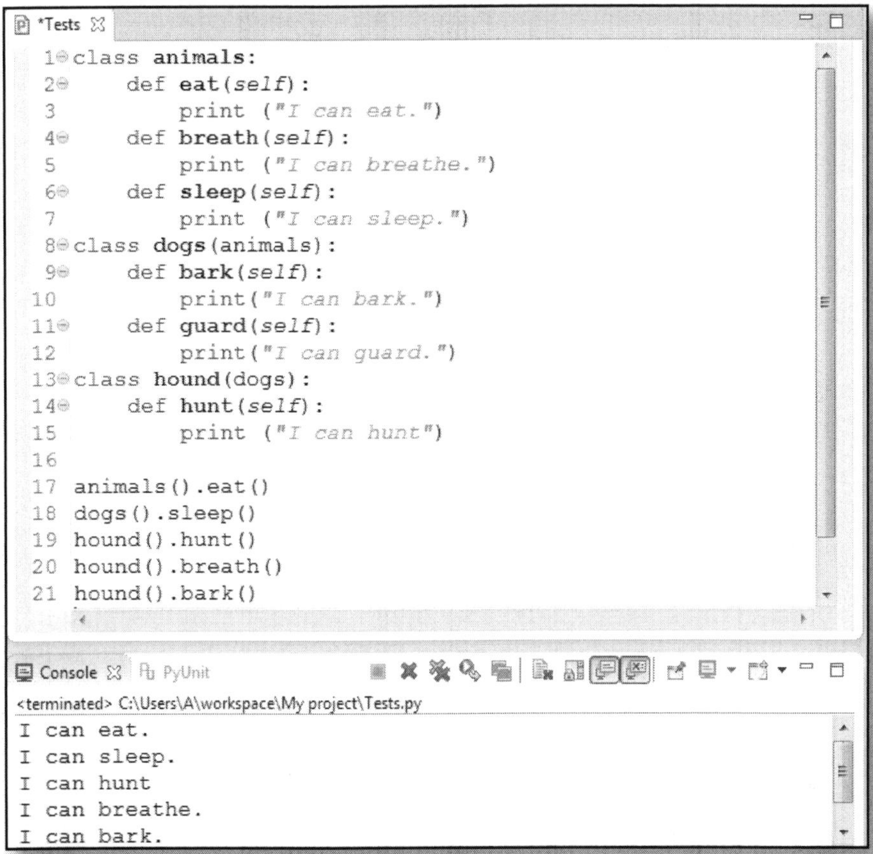

```
1 class animals:
2     def eat(self):
3         print ("I can eat.")
4     def breath(self):
5         print ("I can breathe.")
6     def sleep(self):
7         print ("I can sleep.")
8 class dogs(animals):
9     def bark(self):
10        print("I can bark.")
11    def guard(self):
12        print("I can guard.")
13 class hound(dogs):
14    def hunt(self):
15        print ("I can hunt")
16
17 animals().eat()
18 dogs().sleep()
19 hound().hunt()
20 hound().breath()
21 hound().bark()
```

```
Console      PyUnit
<terminated> C:\Users\A\workspace\My project\Tests.py
I can eat.
I can sleep.
I can hunt
I can breathe.
I can bark.
```

Figure 9.10: Three classes having inheritance connections among them.

CHAPTER 9 LAB EXERCISE

We will create a class that calculates a person's payroll. We will pass in an employee's name, how much they earn per hour, and how many hours they have worked that week. This will then generate a value that we will output.

Let's also create an optional method that will determine whether they worked overtime or not. If they did, for the hours they worked overtime, they get time and a half—their normal hourly rate, plus half of their hourly rate. After these figures have been calculated, print out the employee's name, how many normal hours they work at what wage, and how much money they earned for that. Do the same for the overtime. Finally, print out a total for both added together.

LAB SOLUTION

```python
class Payroll:
    def __init__(self, name):
        self.name = name
        self.hours = 0
        self.overHours = 0
        self.wage = 0
    def setEarnings(self, wage):
        self.wage = wage
    def setHours(self,hours):
        self.hours = hours
    def setOvertime(self,hours = 0):
        self.overHours = hours
    def calculate(self):
        print(self.name , ' worked:')
        print(self.hours , ' normal hours @
' , self.wage , ' for $' , self.hours *
self.wage)
        print(self.overHours , ' overtime
hours @ ' , self.wage * 1.5 , ' for $' ,
self.overHours * 1.5 * self.wage)
        print('Totaling: $' , ((self.
wage*1.5*self.overHours)+ (self.wage*self.
```

```
hours)) , ' for One Weeks work')

person = Payroll('Me')
person.setEarnings(14.20)
person.setHours(4.2)
person.setOvertime(1)
person.calculate()
```

Running this code using my own sample values you would get this result:

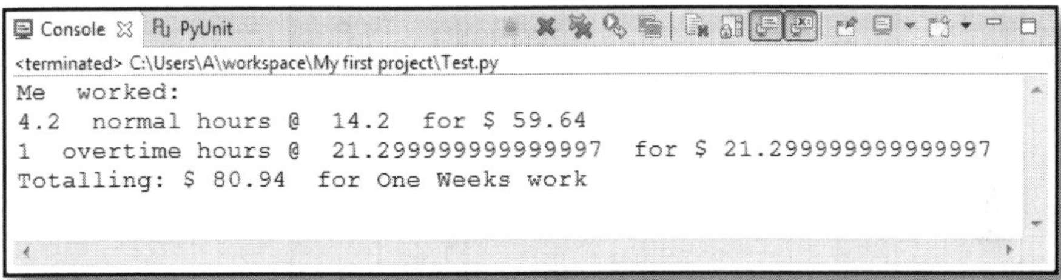

```
Console   PyUnit
<terminated> C:\Users\A\workspace\My first project\Test.py
Me   worked:
4.2   normal hours @   14.2   for $ 59.64
1   overtime hours @   21.299999999999997   for $ 21.299999999999997
Totalling: $ 80.94   for One Weeks work
```

Figure 9.11: The output shows the name of the person and the normal and overtime hours worked and their respective rates together with the total.

CHAPTER SUMMARY

In this chapter you were introduced to classes and the concepts related to them.

You learned the syntax of defining a class and you defined your own class samples and ran them using different instances.

You now know that methods are at the core of a class structure and you know how to access class methods after a class has been defined.
You should have an understanding of the use of keyword arguments and how to store and return data from objects such as dictionaries or tuples within classes.

You learned the inheritance concept and you should now know that inheritance is the functionality you need to use when defining classes that are inherited from larger classes.

In the next chapter, you will learn about file handling by learning how to open, read, and write files that reside in your computer using Python scripting.

CHAPTER 10

FILE HANDLING

CHAPTER OBJECTIVES:

- You will learn how to open the content of a text file inside the Python programming environment.
- You will learn how to read and write the content of a text file into another text file.
- You will learn how to read and write the content of bigger text files.
- You will learn how to read and write different types of files in addition to text files.

10.1 OPENING FILES

So far, we have only been writing programs that process internal information contained within the programming script. We have not been interacting with objects that reside outside the script. In this chapter, we will take an important step and learn how to handle files that reside in your computer file system using Python.

Basically, the two main actions we need to perform when we want to handle files are reading and writing. Both these actions are implemented via the **open** function. In this section we will learn the first action – reading files.

Before we go through some examples to see how the *open* function works, we need to create a sample file in our computer. For this, let's create a new text file. In my case, I created a text file and inserted the section titles of this chapter and saved it in a folder. You are free to save it in any folder you want, but be sure to keep track of the folder path because that is crucial for Python to locate the file. Another thing you need to keep note of is the file name. Here is a screenshot of my file and its location:

Open

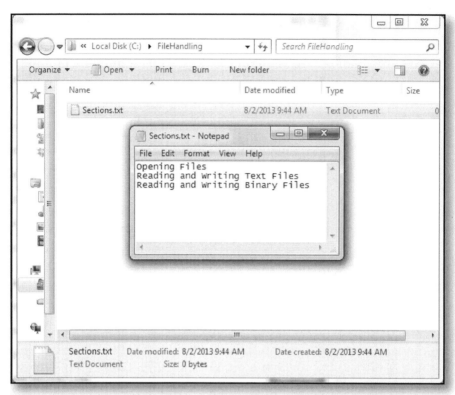

Figure 10.1: Sample text file located in a folder in Windows operating system

Now we will try to open (read) the text contained inside the file in Python. Here is the code that does that:

```python
file = open("C:/FileHandling/Sections.txt")
for line in file:
    print (line)
```

What the function *open* does, is fetch the data contained inside a file. This fetched data is then assigned to a variable. This is exactly what we do in the first line of our code block—we are assigning the data of the *Section.txt* file to our variable named *file*. Notice that you should specify the complete path directory of your file so that Python can locate it.

> **Tip**: If the file you are trying to open resides in the same directory with the Python script you are writing, you do not have to declare the whole path of the directory. In this case, only the file name would be enough for Python to locate the file.

Then, in the second and the third line, we use the *print* function via a *for* loop to display the data contained inside our text file. Notice that we are using the *print* function in the same manner we used to print out lines from an array. The output of the previous code would be this one:

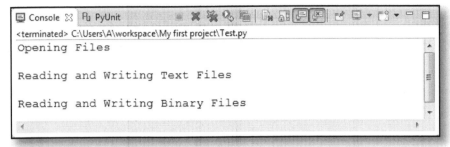

Figure 10.2: Displayed data from an opened text file using the *open* function.

The code we wrote was very basic without having any advanced functionality. You may have noticed that the text lines we displayed are separated by empty lines. To remove these empty lines, we would add an **end** parameter to the *print* function, like this: **End**

```
file = open("C:/FileHandling/Sections.txt")
for line in file:
    print (line, end = "")
```

This time, the output would be slightly different:

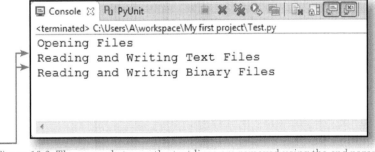

Figure 10.3: The spaces between the text lines are removed using the *end* parameter.

The *end* parameter specifies how the lines contained inside the text file will be separated when displayed via the *print* function. In this case, we set that the lines will not be separated by blank lines. You could put any character you want inside the quotes and the lines will be separated by that character. In this case we did not input any character separator.

10.2 READING AND WRITING TEXT FILES

In the previous section you were given an introduction explaining how to interact with files via Python scripting. We used the *open* function in the previous section using only one parameter, the file location path. In that default one-parameter mode, the function worked as a reader of the text file. So, it read and printed out the text that the file contained. In this section you will learn how to write text inside a text file. This is done by adding a second parameter to the *open* function. Before we write the code that does that, we need to create an empty text file where text will be written. I will create one, name it *New.txt* and put it in the same directory where I have the *Sections.txt* file that I used in the previous section. You also need to have your sample file which you used along with me in section 10.1.

The idea here is that we are going to fetch the text contained inside the *Section.txt* file and put it inside the *New.txt* file. Here is the code that does that:

```
input = open("C:/FileHandling/Sections.
txt","r")
output = open("C:/FileHandling/New.
txt","w")
for line in input:
    print (line, file = output, end = "")
```

In the first line we are fetching the text from *Sections.txt* and assigning it to the variable *input*. The parameter *r* indicates that we are reading the content of the file. This is the same thing we did in the examples of the previous section. The use of *r* is optional. The default action that the *open* function does when used with one parameter is reading the file. However, in this case we decided to use the *r* parameter as just a matter of style.

You do not have this freedom when you want to write inside a file. In this case you have to use the *w* parameter to let the program know what you want to write inside the file. This is exactly what we do in the second line of our code. Then, in the third and fourth lines we complete the writing process. Notice the similarity of these lines with the lines we used to print out the text in the examples from the previous section. The crucial difference here is the insertion of another parameter inside the *print* function, which is *file = output*. This parameter tells the program to insert the content inside a file. This file is represented by the variable output which contains the New.txt file path location. After running this code, go to the folder where your New.txt file resides and open it to see if the content has been written inside. You will have something similar to this:

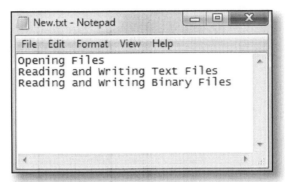

Figure 10.4: Text file after the content has been written using the *open* function with the *w* parameter.

Tip: If you want to add the content of a text file below some existing content of another text file, you must use the *a* parameter instead of *w*. The *a* parameter stands for append and it will append the content instead of overwriting it.

In the example we just used, we had to deal with only three lines of text and the code we used does the job perfectly. However, if the number of text lines inside the text file was significantly higher, our code would have trouble processing it because the *for* loop we are using would have to go through every line one by one. If you were to handle bigger text files having a considerable amount of lines, we would suggest another approach. Let's go through this and handle a real life text file that contains more than 30 thousand lines of text. This is how a part of the file looks:

```
buffersize = 1000000
input = open('C:/FileHandling/BigFile.txt','r')
output = open('C:/FileHandling/New.txt', 'w')
buffer = input.read(buffersize)

while len(buffer):
    output.write(buffer)
    print('.', end='')
    buffer = input.read(buffersize)
```

Figure 10.5: A big text file that has to be read and written using a buffer

You can create your own big text file by simply copying some big text inside an empty text file. Give a name such as *BigFile.txt* and save it in a folder. You do not need to create an empty new file (where the text will be written) manually because this will be created by the code.

To work with this big file in Python, this time we will be using a **buffer** instead of the *for* loop. A *buffer* provides a faster way to read and write a text file because it reads and writes the data by big groups of text. This technique works on a byte basis—it reads and writes the content of the file by accessing groups of bytes. In our case, the code we would use to write all the text from one file to another is:

Buffer

```
buffersize = 1000000
input = open('    C:/FileHandling/BigFile.
txt','r')
output = open('C:/FileHandling/New.txt',
'w')
buffer = input.read(buffersize)

while len(buffer):
output.write(buffer)
print('.', end='')
buffer = input.read(buffersize)
```

First, we create a variable and assign it the number of bytes that the reading algorithm will be stepping through. In this case, the algorithm will access groups of 1 million bytes of data. The whole file has a size of 9,351,168 bytes.

Then, in the second and third lines, we create one file input and one file output variable with the respective read and write capabilities. In the fourth line, we create a buffer object that will store the output based on the buffer size we specified previously.

Then we move on to the next block which is a while loop. This loop will iterate through text buffers and write them to the output file. As the writing continues, we are printing out some dots where every dot represents a written buffersize of 1,000,000 bytes:

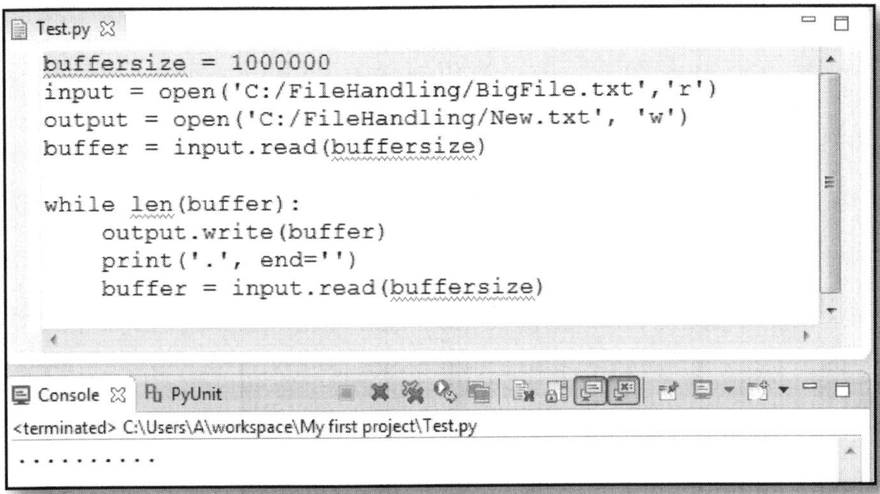

```
📄 Test.py ✕                                          ▭ 🗗
   buffersize = 1000000
   input = open('C:/FileHandling/BigFile.txt','r')
   output = open('C:/FileHandling/New.txt', 'w')
   buffer = input.read(buffersize)

   while len(buffer):
       output.write(buffer)
       print('.', end='')
       buffer = input.read(buffersize)

 ◄                                                    ►

🖥 Console ✕   🐍 PyUnit        ▪ ✖ ❋ ☙ ▤ | 🖹 🗚 🗐🗷 🗗 🖵 ▾ 🗂 ▾ ▭ 🗖
<terminated> C:\Users\A\workspace\My first project\Test.py
. . . . . . . . . .                                                ▲
```

Figure 10.6: Reading and writing a text file using a buffer and a while loop

The number of dots is the number of written buffers. In this case, we had 10 dots because 9,351,168 bytes make up nine groups of one million bytes each and one last group with the rest of the bytes. Notice that it processed very quickly. Reading and writing all the lines one by one would take a considerable amount of time. After you run the code, check the *New.txt* to see if the text has been written inside. The two text files must have the same content.

10.3 READING AND WRITING BINARY FILES

In the two previous sections we worked with reading and writing text files only. In this section, we will learn how to read and write files that are not of text type. No matter what type a file is, it is always made up of bytes. Therefore, we will use the buffer technique we used previously, but this time we will work with a .jpg picture file such as this:

The code is mostly the same with some minor changes:

Figure 10.7: Picture file to be read and written using the buffer technique.

```
buffersize = 1000000
input = open('C:/
FileHandling/Python.jpg','rb')
output = open('C:/FileHandling/NewPython.
jpg', 'wb')
buffer = input.read(buffersize)

while len(buffer):
output.write(buffer)
print('.', end='')
buffer = input.read(buffersize)
```

Here, again we are using a buffer size of one million bytes. So, the reading and writing will be done every one million bytes. In the second and third lines we set the input location and file name. Notice here that we are using the *rb* and *wb* parameters where *rb* stands for read binary and *wb* for write binary. These are the parameters to be used when the files are not text files. The while block is the same block we used in the example of section 10.2. So, the only conceptual difference of this code from the previous one we used with text files, is the use of binary parameters for the *open* function *rb* and *wb*.

QUESTIONS FOR REVIEW

1. What does the following code do?

```
file = open("Sections.txt")
for i in file:
    print (i)
```

   a. Prints out the *i* character contained inside the *Sections.txt* file.
   b. Prints out the content of *Sections.txt* on a line by line basis.
   c. Creates a file called *Sections.txt*.
   d. The code will not work due to syntax errors.

2. Why do we set a big buffer size number?
   a. To have the code run more quickly.
   b. To have a big number of iterations.
   c. To have a consistent number of lines.
   d. To have the bytes printed out correctly.

3. What is not true about the buffer technique?
   a. It is used to have a quicker execution of the code.
   b. It works with all types of files.
   c. It accesses the content on a byte basis.
   d. It works better with text files.

CHAPTER 10 LAB EXERCISE

Your task is to create a class called *LogMessage*. This class will have three functions. The first function is the initial *__init__()* method, which will take one parameter—the filename for the file. The second is the *read()* method, which will output all of the content from that text file. The third is the *write()* method, which will take one input—the message that you wish to write in append mode to the text file.

Your *read()* and *write()* should use appropriate settings to either read or write (write should append to the text file) to make sure that you don't receive errors.

```
class LogMessage:
def __init__(self,filename):
self.filename = filename
def read(self):
        f = open(self.filename,'r')
lines = f.readlines()
for each in lines:
print(each, end='')
def write(self,message):
        f = open(self.filename, 'a')
f.write(message)

log = LogMessage('test.txt')
log.write('Testing...' + '\n')
log.write('test123' + '\n')
log.read()
```

This is how the solution would look in Eclipse:

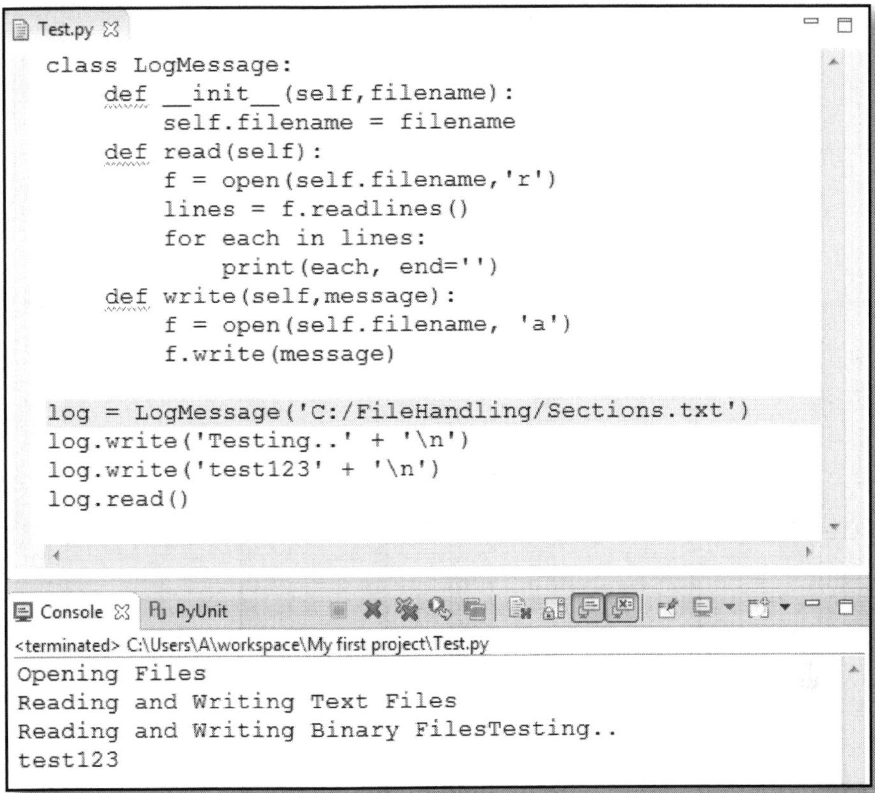

```
Test.py

class LogMessage:
    def __init__(self,filename):
        self.filename = filename
    def read(self):
        f = open(self.filename,'r')
        lines = f.readlines()
        for each in lines:
            print(each, end='')
    def write(self,message):
        f = open(self.filename, 'a')
        f.write(message)

log = LogMessage('C:/FileHandling/Sections.txt')
log.write('Testing..' + '\n')
log.write('test123' + '\n')
log.read()
```

```
Console    PyUnit
<terminated> C:\Users\A\workspace\My first project\Test.py
Opening Files
Reading and Writing Text Files
Reading and Writing Binary FilesTesting..
test123
```

Figure 10.8: Lab solution with the output after the sample file has been processed.

CHAPTER SUMMARY

In this chapter you were introduced to the concepts of file handling. You learned how to access text files from the Python programming environment.

You worked with reading and writing text files using the *open* function and the *for* loop by accessing the content line by line.

You also worked with the *while* loop by accessing the content on a byte basis and you understood when to use the *for* loop and when to use the *while* loop.

We discussed the buffer technique and you learned how to read and write file types that are not text files and you should now know how to use the proper parameters for reading and writing binary files.

In the next chapter, you will learn about database handling, which is a similar file handling.

CHAPTER 11

DATABASE HANDLING

CHAPTER OBJECTIVES:

- You will learn how to interact with a database from within Python by creating database files, database tables, and building table structures.
- You will learn how to insert and update records in database tables.
- You will learn how to query database data by retrieving records and using their values for various operations in Python.
- You will learn how to delete existing table records.

11.1 CREATING THE DATABASE

Python, like many other computer languages, is able to interact with a **database,** which is a collection of information organized to provide efficient access by computer programs. Python can access a *database* through its specialized libraries. While there are a few libraries that enable the interaction between Python and databases, in this book we will work with the **SQLite3** library. *SQLite3* is a set of Python scripts that contain already-made functions which enable the interaction with a database. This library must have been automatically installed along with Eclipse, so you don't have to install it separately.

> This chapter uses:
> **SQLite3**

The first thing we will do in Python is create an empty database file. This is a very easy task accomplished by the following code:

```
import SQLite3
db = SQLite3.connect('database1.db')
```

First, we need to import the *SQLite3* library in Python. This is done using the **import** command along with the name of the library. Once we import it inside our program, we can use the library and its built-in functions as many times as we want. In the second line we make a connection to a database. In this example, the name of the database is database1.db. If this database

> **import**

file exists in your system, a connection will be established. Otherwise, a new empty database file named database1.db will be created and simultaneously a connection with it will be established. After you run this code, try to locate the newly created database file on the PyDev package explorer panel by refreshing it first:

Figure 11.1: Database file created using the *SQLite3* library.

All we did so far was create an empty database file and established a connection with it. Now, we are going to create a table inside the created database that is constructed by fields. To do that, we need to write some code inside Python, using the **SQL** language.

> *SQL* is a programming language designed to manage data held in databases. Through the *slqlite3* library, Python allows *SQL* code to be written inside its environment.

Here is the complete code that creates two tables with three fields each:

```
import SQLite3
db = SQLite3.connect('database.db')

db.execute('create table person (firstname
text, secondname text, age int)')
db.execute('create table book (title text,
author text, genre text)')
```

Notice that the first two lines remain the same. Then, in the second and the third lines we create the tables *person* and *book* respectively. The key tool to create the tables here is the **execute()** method which is attached after the database object (*db*) we created earlier. The *execute()* method executes *SQL* code inside Python. Therefore, all the code we write inside the parenthesis following *execute()* is *SQL* code.

execute()

Let's take a closer look at the first *SQL* statement contained within the *execute()* method:

```
'create table person (firstname text,
secondname text, age int)'
```

Here we tell the program to create a table named *person*. Then we create three fields, one named *firstname* that will hold text values, one named *secondname* that will again hold text values, and another one named *age* that holds integer values. This way, the table and its structure is created. Similarly, the other *execute()* method creates the table called *book*. After you run the whole code, try to open the "database1.db" file inside eclipse to see how it looks.

Tip: If you do not have any database system installed on your computer, you might not see any meaningful result when you open the database file. However, the database is stored in the correct structure.

The code we just wrote runs without problem if the database file is empty (free of tables), but if this is not the case, you may run into overwriting problems. To avoid this, we should add two other lines inside our code.

Therefore a safer code to create the tables would be this one:

```
import SQLite3
db = SQLite3.connect('database1.db')

db.execute('drop table if exists person')
db.execute('create table person (firstname
text, secondname text, age int)')
db.execute('drop table if exists book')
db.execute('create table people (firstname
text, secondname text, age int)')
```

The lines we added will overwrite the existing tables within the database file with the new ones as created by the code. In the next section, we will populate the tables with sample data.

1. What does the *import SQLite3* command do?
   a. Imports tables inside Python.
   b. Imports SQL methods inside Python.
   c. Imports a library that is able to handle interactions with a database.
   d. Imports a library that creates a database system.

2. What argument does the *execute()* method take?
   a. Python executable commands.
   b. Table fields.
   c. SQL data types.
   d. SQL code.

 LAB ACTIVITY

Create a new table within the existing database. Name the table "triangle", and add three fields, "type", "area" and "rightTriangle". Try to assign the appropriate types for each of the fields.

LAB SOLUTION

```
import SQLite3
db = SQLite3.connect('database1.db')
db.execute('create table triangle (type
text, area float, rightTriangle boolean)')
```

11.2 INSERTING AND UPDATING RECORDS

In the previous section, we created two empty tables. In this section, we are going to insert some **records** into one of these tables.

A *record-* also called a **row** or **tuple** in the database domain, is a set of data that have the same structure in the table. In order to insert records, we need an existing table. Therefore, make sure you have the tables we created previously inside the database file. They provide the structure for the records that are about to be inserted.

record

Now, we will insert a record inside the table *person* that consists of three table cells. Each cell will fill one occurrence for each of the three fields – *firstname*, *secondname* and *age*. Here is the code that inserts the record:

```
import SQLite3

db = SQLite3.connect('database1.db')
db.execute('insert into person (firstname,
secondname, age) values ("John",
"Smith",25)')
db.commit()
```

Running this, a first record will be inserted inside the "database1.db" file. You should be familiar with the first two lines which are identical to the code example from the previous section. Then, in the third line, we have the *execute()* method with its *SQL* code arguments inside its parentheses. In this line we insert the values "John" in the *firstname* field, "Smith" in the *secondname* field, and "25" in the *age* field. To execute the whole process, you need to add a *commit()* method at the end of the code. If you now open the "database1.db" file, you should see that some values have been added. To have a structured view, you would need a database management software which is specialized to handle database files.

You might come across scenarios where you want to alter some particular records. Here is an example where we change the age of John Smith from 25 to 35:

```
import SQLite3

db = SQLite3.connect('database1.db')
db.execute('update person set age = 35
where secondname = "Smith"')
db.commit()
```

Notice how the argument inside the *execute()* method changes. In this case, we used the *update SQL* keyword instead of *insert*. We may have many records within a table, therefore, we have to include a reference of the record we want to update. In this case the reference is the *secondname* field. That means we are updating only the record where the *secondname* field is equal to "John".

In the same way, you can insert and update other records from any existing table that resides inside your database file. In the next section, you will be learning querying operations such as retrieving and deleting records.

 QUESTIONS FOR REVIEW

1. Which of the following is not a SQL keyword?
   a. set
   b. insert
   c. update
   d. execute()

2. What would you do to change an existing record from a table?
   a. Use the update keyword.
   b. Add a new record.
   c. Use the *commit()* command.
   d. A record cannot be changed.

LAB ACTIVITY

Insert a new record inside the existing table "book" using the information from your favorite book.

LAB SOLUTION

```
import SQLite3

db = SQLite3.connect('database1.db')
db.execute('insert into book (title,
author, genre) values ("Gulliver\'s
Travels", "Jonathan Swift","Fantasy")')
db.commit()
```

11.3 RETRIEVING AND DELETING RECORDS

In the first part of this section we will retrieve or fetch data from the database we have created. This retrieved data will be the records we added previously to our tables. By fetching this data, we are able to use it inside our Python script for various operations. In the following example we will fetch all the data that table *person* contains and we will print it out using the Python *print* command. Here is the example:

```
import SQLite3

db = SQLite3.connect('database1.db')
table = db.execute('select * from person')
for i in table:
    print(i)
```

Again, whenever we need to interact with a database, the appropriate library has to be called using the *import* command. Then, a connection with the database is established. In the third line, we create a variable called *table* that will hold the table data. This is called a **cursor** object and it holds data that has a database format. As with the previous examples, inside the *execute()* method, we had to write *SQL* code. This time using *SQL* we select all (*) the data from table *person*.

cursor

At this point, we have fetched that data and stored it inside the *table* variable. Now, we can do whatever we want with it. In this case, we are printing it out using a *for* loop. The *for* loop will access the data on a *record* basis—it will print out the records one by one. When you run this code, you shall get this result:

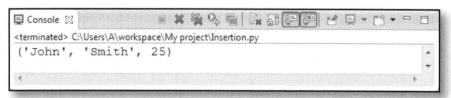

Figure 11.2: Fetching all the records from a database table.

This way, we have retrieved the data from a database and used it within Python. In this example we retrieved all the data, but sometimes you might want to select only the records of some specific fields within a table such as *firstname* and *secondname* for example, and not the age. In this case, you would not use the asterisk (*) symbol:

```
import SQLite3

db = SQLite3.connect('database1.db')
table = db.execute('select firstname,
secondname from person')
for i in table:
    print(i)
```

Notice that this time we explicitly declared what fields we want to fetch the records from. Here is the result:

```
Console ☒                    ■ ✕ ✖ ☊ ➡ | ➡ ▦ ➡ ➡ | ➡ ➡ ▾ ➡ ▾ ▬ ⬜
<terminated> C:\Users\A\workspace\My project\Insertion.py
('John', 'Smith')
```

Figure 11.3: Fetching specific field records from a database table.

Sometimes, you might want to have the table field names attached to every record value. In this case, we would go for a dictionary approach in Python. To do that, you need to activate **row_factory** which is a function of *slqite3* that enables the retrieval of the data in form of a dictionary. Here is the code that fetches and displays the records with their field names attached in a dictionary format:

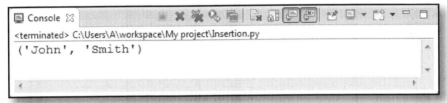

row_factory

```
import SQLite3

db = SQLite3.connect('database1.db')
db.row_factory = SQLite3.Row
table = db.execute('select * from person')
for i in table:
    print(dict(i))
```

And the result is this:

```
Console ⌗
<terminated> C:\Users\A\workspace\My project\Insertion.py
{'firstname': 'John', 'age': 25, 'secondname': 'Smith'}
```

Figure 11.4: Fetching table records in form of a dictionary.

One more database operation that is important to learn is the **delete** operation, which is used to delete records from a database table. *Delete* is used in a similar fashion as with the other commands. Here is an example where we delete a record from the database:

delete

```python
import SQLite3

db = SQLite3.connect('database1.db')
table = db.execute('delete from person
where secondname = "Smith"')
db.commit()
for i in table:
    print(i)
```

Notice that the code is mostly the same as the previous ones. The only thing that changes is the *SQL* part. Here we are telling the program to delete the row that meets the criteria after the *where* clause, which consists of the record where the second name is "Smith".

Learning these commands enables you to have a clear understanding of the interaction between Python and a database.

QUESTIONS FOR REVIEW

1. What command do we use to retrieve database records?
   a. select
   b. *
   c. get()
   d. execute()

2. Why would we use a dictionary when retrieving records from a database?

  a. Because there is no other way.

  b. To keep a copy of the records within Python.

  c. For no specific reason.

  d. To have the record values attached to their field names.

LAB ACTIVITY

Retrieve and print out the record you inserted into table *book* in the lab activity from section 11.2.

LAB SOLUTION

```
import SQLite3

db = SQLite3.connect('database1.db')
table = db.execute('select * from book')
for i in table:
    print(i)
```

In my case, the result would look like this in Eclipse:

```
1 import sqlite3
2
3 db = sqlite3.connect('database1.db')
4 table = db.execute('select * from book')
5 for i in table:
6     print(i)
```

```
Console ☒
<terminated> C:\Users\A\workspace\My project\Tests.py
("Guliver's travels", 'Jonathan Swift', 'Fantasy')
```

Figure 11. 5: Retrieving a record from table *book*.

Your task is to recreate the class from the previous chapters' lab, and use a database instead of a flat file. This will then have three functions. The first is the initial _init_() method, which will take one parameter of the name of the database. The second is a *read()* method, which will output all of the content from that database in ascending order. The third is a *write()* method, which will take one input, which is the message that you wish to write to the database.

Your *read()* and *write()* should use appropriate *SQLite3* commands to write or read from a database. Remember, a database needs a name and a table inside of it with one field for the message.

After this is done, you can import this into any previous task, and where we output an error message, you can also store that in the database.

LAB SOLUTION

```
import SQLite3
class LogMessage:
    def __init__(self,dbname):
        self.dbname = dbname
        db = SQLite3.connect(self.dbname)
        db.execute('create table if not
exists LogMessage (message)')
        db.commit()
        db.close()
    def read(self):
        db = SQLite3.connect(self.dbname)
        data = db.execute('select * from
LogMessage')
        for each in data:
            print(each)
        db.close()
    def write(self,message):
        db = SQLite3.connect(self.dbname)
        db.execute('insert into LogMessage
```

```
(message) values (?)', (message,))
        db.commit()
        db.close()

log = LogMessage('test.db')
log.write('Testing')
log.write('Test')
log.read()
```

This is how the solution and the output look in Eclipse:

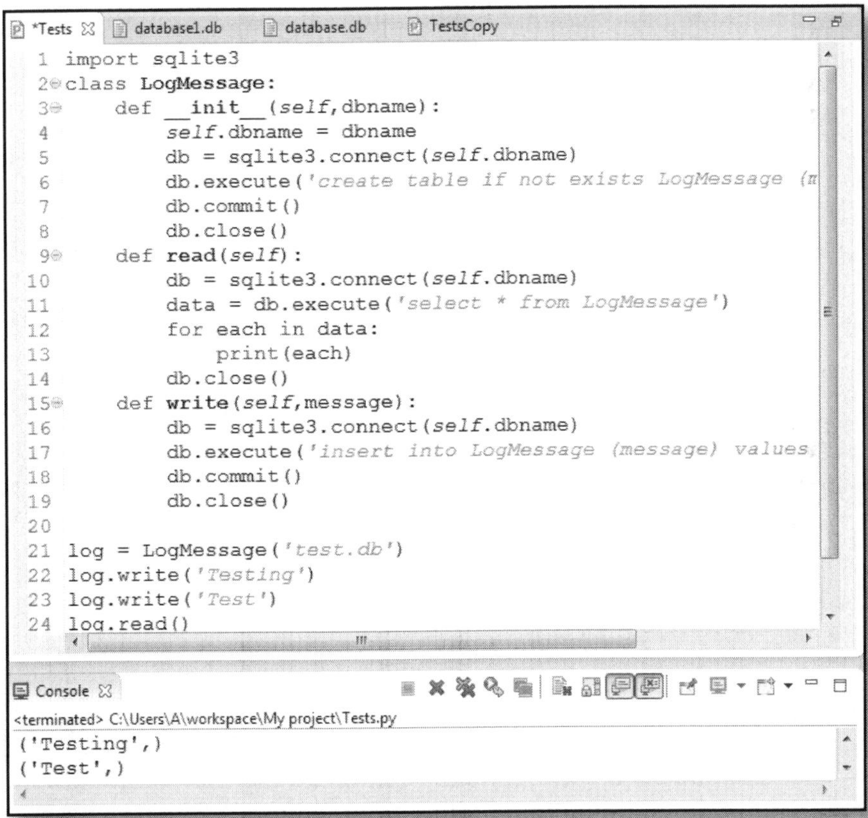

Figure 11.6: Creating a class that interacts with a database.

Chapter Summary

In this chapter, you learned how to interact with a database from within Python and how to create a database file where database structured data can be stored.

Using examples, you practiced creating new tables within the database and structured those tables with new fields with appropriate data types, while also learning how to insert new records inside an existing table and also how to update existing records inside a table.

You were introduced to the technique of retrieving data from a database table in order to use them within Python. You were able to store these data within various Python data types such as tuples and dictionaries.
You also learned how to delete existing records from a table.

In the next chapter, you will learn about modules, how to use and create them.

CHAPTER 12

MODULES

CHAPTER OBJECTIVES:

- You will learn what standard libraries are.
- You will learn how to use standard libraries within your programs and how to get information about all Python standard libraries.
- You will learn how and when to use the *datetime* and *sys* libraries.
- You will learn how to create modules and use them in your programs.

12.1 USING STANDARD LIBRARIES

Python has many importable libraries which are a collection of modules designed to be used in different programming scenarios and tasks. Some of these libraries are distributed along with Python—that means you do not have to install them separately. These libraries are referred to as **standard libraries**.

This chapter uses:
Database & Sys

 Standard libraries contain built-in modules that provide many additional components to the language.

An example of a standard library is *sqlite3* which we mastered in chapter 11. For a full list of the standard libraries along with their documentations, see http://docs.python.org/2/library/.

Tip: Remember that in order to access the functionality of a library you should first import it inside your script using the import command along with the library name.

 In this chapter, we will work with two standard libraries. The first one is the **datetime** library. *datetime* is a collection of modules that support manipulation of date and time data.

Let's now take a look at an example of the functionality provided by the *datetime* library. As you write your new programs, for various reasons you might need to have a current date and time that will be incorporated with your other data. Here is the code that would provide the date and time of every given moment:

```
import datetime
dt = datetime.datetime.now()
print (dt)
```

As you already know, in the first line, we first have to import the library in order to use its functionality. Then, in the second line we create a variable called *dt*. The *dt* variable contains the output value of the **now()** function which is the function that generates the current date and time. Function *now()* is 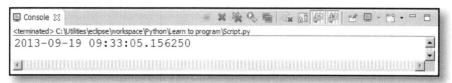 contained inside a class called **datetime**. Therefore, the way we call this function is *datetime.now()*. The *datetime* class itself is contained within the **datetime** library. So, the complete expression is *datetime.datetime. now()*. To sum it up we can say that function *now()* belongs to the *datetime* class which belongs to the *datetime* library.

Here is the expected result:

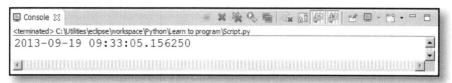

Figure 12.1: Current (at the time of the code execution) date and time

Notice that the timestamp you get back is very precise. This may come in handy sometimes. A very general example of the time functionality, no matter what kind of program you are building, would be when you want to test different blocks of your code to see which runs slower than it should.

Suppose you had a big program that takes a lot of time to run and you want to know which part of it is causing the delay. In this case, the *datetime* library functionality would become very useful.

In such a case, you would wrap blocks of your code within current time functions and calculate the difference from the time the block of code starts running to the time the running ends. Suppose one of the code blocks inside your program is a while loop. In this case, we would use the current time function like this:

```
import datetime
i=0
start = datetime.datetime.now()

while i<1000000:
    i=i+1

end = datetime.datetime.now()
print (end-start)
```

> **Tip**: Remember that the code in Python is executed starting from the top of the script and going down to the bottom line, executing every line one by one.

In our code, we start by importing the *datetime* library. We also create a variable with an initial value of zero. Then, we create another variable that will store the current time which coincides with the time the while loop block will be executed. The next two lines are the while loop block. The action that the while loop will perform is adding one to variable *i* starting from zero and up to one million. Immediately after the while loop execution ends, another variable called *end* will store the current time, which is the time the while loop execution finishes. Then we just need to print out the difference between the end and the start time to see how much time it took for the while loop to finish its action.

Depending on your computer parameters, you might get a different value than mine:

Figure 12.2: Time needed for the while loop to be executed.

In my case, the time interval was around 0.31 seconds. You can try to experiment and test the execution time of other codes you have learned throughout this book.

Another library we will be looking up today is the **sys** library. It provides access to some variables used or maintained by the interpreter and also to functions that interact strongly with the interpreter. You can find it in the list of Python libraries from the link we provided previously.

Like every library, the *sys* library has many functions. Here we will work with one of them – **path**, which returns a list of strings that specifies the search path for modules. The list also contains the directory path of the current project. Here is how we use it:

path

```
import sys
print (sys.path)
```

First we import the library and then we access one of its functions – *path* by printing out its output. Simple enough, right?

In my case, I get this result:

Figure 12.3: A list of strings of different project relevant paths.

You might use this function when you need to know or use the directory of your project or the modules.

These were just a few standard library functions. As you program with Python, new needs may arise for other functions. In that case, the standard library list under http://docs.python.org/2/library/ is a good place to look for information.

QUESTIONS FOR REVIEW

1. What is the first step when you want to use a library inside Python?
   a. Import the *sys.path*.
   b. Import the library.
   c. Print out the library.
   d. Assign the library to a variable.

2. Which of the following would correctly print out the current date and time?
   a. print (datetime)
   b. print (datetime.datetime(now))
   c. print datetime.now()
   d. print (datetime.datetime.now())

LAB ACTIVITY

Try to print out the day of the week using the *datetime* library.

   Hint: Use the weekday() function and be aware that the days in Python are defined with numbers starting from zero for Monday, to six for Sunday.

LAB SOLUTION

```
import datetime
dt = datetime.datetime.now()
print (datetime.datetime.weekday(dt))
```

Here is the output I received from it:

Figure 12.4: Three printed out indicating that the day of the week is Thursday.

12.2 CREATING A MODULE

In Python, every script that you write can also be used as a module. This module can be imported using the import command just as you did with libraries. To create a module and import it into an empty script file, we first need to create two empty Python scripts in Eclipse. You should create both of them under the same Eclipse project. I will call one of them "SampleModule.py" and start writing some code inside it:

```
def greeting():
    print ("Hello, this is a module
function")
x = "This is a module variable"
```

You should be able to easily understand this code. We have just written a function that prints out some text when called, and we have assigned a string to a variable.

Save the "SampleModule.py" file and open the other Python file you created. You can name this file "SampleModuleTest.py". In this empty file, you can now import the new module whose name is defined by the script name, *SampleModule*. Then you are free to use all its functionality. In this example we can use its variable and function:

```
import SampleModule
SampleModule.greeting()
print(SampleModule.x)
```

First, we imported the module, and then in the second line we called its function. In the third line we print out the value held by variable *x*. The result of the execution would be:

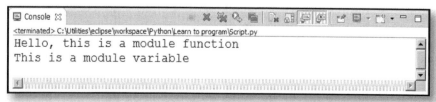

Figure 12.5: Generated output after content of the module is called.

The module functionality enables better organization when writing big programs as it allows the programmer to separate the code into different modules making it more readable and organized.

QUESTIONS FOR REVIEW

1. What is not true about modules?
   a. Collections of modules can form libraries.
   b. Modules are script files.
   c. Modules can be called from other modules.
   d. Choosing to work with modules is just a matter of style.

2. What does the following line of code from the previous example do?

```
SampleModule.greeting()
```

   a. It executes the module *SampleModule.greeting()*.
   b. It creates the function *greeting()* within the module.
   c. It creates an instance of the *greeting()* function.
   d. It calls the function *greeting()* contained in *SampleModule*.

LAB ACTIVITY

While in an empty string, import all the components of the module *SampleModule* in such a way that you will not have to reference the module name any time you want to call an object.

> Tip: Make use of an asterisk. (*)

LAB SOLUTION

```
from SampleModule import *
greeting()
print(x)
```

Here is how the solution and the output look in Eclipse:

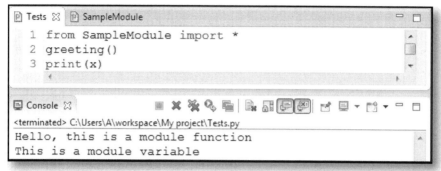

Figure 12.6: Calling all module components waives the need to reference the module name every time.

CHAPTER 12 LAB EXERCISE

We have created two versions of logging messages: first we created a database, and then a file system. With the use of modules, we can combine these two together and have them accessible both at the same time, so we can choose which to use in a program. To do this, combine them both into one file.

To import one or the other, you can do the following:

```
from modulename import   classname
```

That will import the relevant class and will allow you to use the class as it is written inside the script. If you need to use the other class, you can simply change *classname* to the other class, and the database name to the filename, and everything should work.

To test this, create the module LogMessage and then import it into a previous lab exercise and test them both out. They should both work.

LAB SOLUTION

```python
import sqlite3
class LogMessageDB:

    def __init__(self,dbname):
        self.dbname = dbname
        db = sqlite3.connect(self.dbname)
        db.execute('create table if not
exists LogMessage (message)')
        db.commit()
        db.close()
    def read(self):
        db = sqlite3.connect(self.dbname)
        data = db.execute('select * from
LogMessage')
        for each in data:
            print(each)
```

```
            db.close()
    def write(self,message):
        db = sqlite3.connect(self.dbname)
        db.execute('insert into LogMessage
(message) values (?)', (message,))
        db.commit()
        db.close()

class LogMessageFile:
    def __init__(self,filename):
        self.filename = filename
    def read(self):
        f = open(self.filename,'r')
        lines = f.readlines()
        for each in lines:
            print(each, end='')
    def write(self,message):
        f = open(self.filename, 'a')
        f.write(message)
```

CHAPTER SUMMARY

In this chapter, you were introduced to standard libraries that
Python offers to expand the programming functionality. You
now know that when you need extended functionality beyond the
built-in modules that Python offers by default, you should look for
standard libraries and import them inside your program.

You worked with the *datetime* library and learned how to use it
to test the execution time of your programs allowing you to find
delaying obstacles inside your big programs.
You learned about the *sys* library which provided information
about directory paths.
You created your own module and used its functionality inside
script files.

In the next chapter you will learn about debugging your programs.

Chapter 13

DEBUGGING

CHAPTER OBJECTIVES:

- You will learn how to detect syntax errors and be able to understand where they occur in the script.
- You will learn how to debug detected errors and free your code from them.
- You will learn how to detect errors at run time that suspend the program from completely executing and debug them for getting the expected output.

13.1 DEALING WITH SYNTAX ERRORS

It is very common to run into different types of errors while writing programs. The Python interpreter does its best to let you know the type of the error and where it is located.

In this final chapter, we will discuss the most common type of errors: **syntax errors**.

 Syntax errors are errors that emerge due to language and expression syntax that was written incorrectly by the programmer. To see an example of syntax errors, run the following code inside Eclipse:

```python
name = 'John'
if name = 'John'
print('Your name is John')

i = 5
j = 15
k = ((i*j) + (j+i)

    print(k)
```

First we assign the string 'John' to the variable *name* and then we make a test using the *if* statement to see if the variable's value is equal to "John" and print out some text if the test succeeds. Then, we create two variables, *i* and *j*, assign values to them, do some math operations and print out the returned output.

However, running this code returns an error:

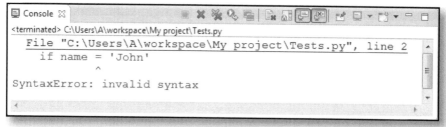

Figure 13.1: A syntax error detected at the second line around the assignment operator.

Read the issued error carefully. In the first line of the error (displayed in blue), the interpreter lets you know that there is an error in the second line of your code. This corresponds to the line if *name* = 'John'. Moreover, you notice an arrow marker (^) which is pointing towards the assignment sign (=). This arrow means that you should review your code at that part. The job of the interpreter ends here, and now it is your turn to look at the part of the code as guided by the interpreter.

If you remember from previous chapters, the assignment operator (=) is actually used to assign a value to a variable—it is not an equal sign. If you want to test whether something is equal to something else, you should use the equal sign (==) which is a like a double assignment operator. Keeping this in mind, we correct our code as follows:

```
name = 'John'
if name == 'John'
print('Your name is John')

i = 5
j = 15
k = ((i*j) + (j+i)

    print(k)
```

Even though we corrected the error that was pointed out, we still get another error when we run this code:

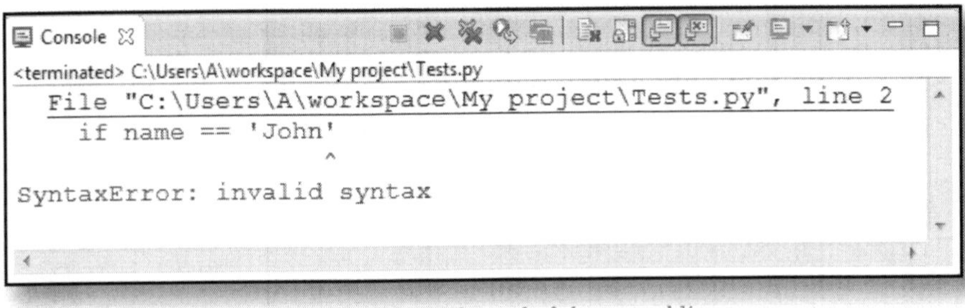
Console
<terminated> C:\Users\A\workspace\My project\Tests.py
File "C:\Users\A\workspace\My project\Tests.py", line 2
if name == 'John'
^
SyntaxError: invalid syntax

Figure 13.2: A syntax error is detected at the end of the second line.

Notice that we still have an error at the second line, but this time at the end of it. The interpreter does its best and gives us the approximate location of the error. Now, you need to take another cautious look at the code, and you should be able to realize that a colon (:) meant to be at the end of an *if* statement is missing. After you add the colon, the code should look like this:

```
name = 'John'
if name == 'John':
print('Your name is John')

i = 5
j = 15
k = ((i*j) + (j+i)

    print(k)
```

Running the code again, you will come across another syntax problem:

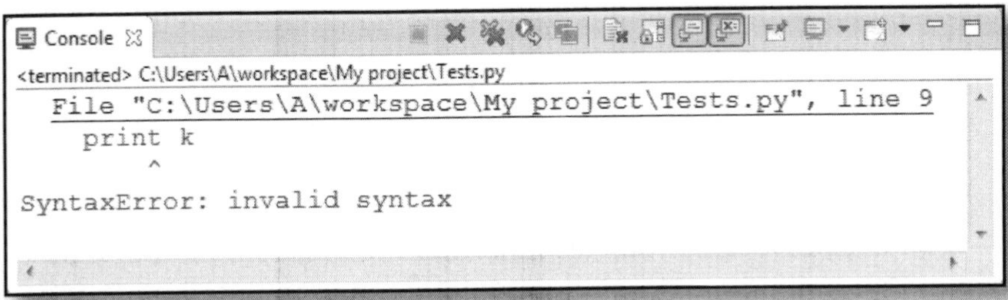
Console
<terminated> C:\Users\A\workspace\My project\Tests.py
File "C:\Users\A\workspace\My project\Tests.py", line 9
print k
^
SyntaxError: invalid syntax

Figure 13.3: A syntax error is detected at the ninth line around the *print* function.

This time, the error occurred at the ninth line. Here is where you have to be more cautious because this time the interpreter is giving a rough estimation—the error is not exactly on the line where the arrow marker is pointing. This time, you should look at the expression that comes before the print command. This corresponds to this line:

```
k = ((i*j) + (j+i)
```

Notice that a bracket is missing at the end of the line. Go ahead and add it:

```
name = 'John'
if name == 'John':
print('Your name is John')

i = 5
j = 15
k = ((i*j) + (j+i))

    print(k)
```

Once you have added the missing bracket and ran the code, you should get this result:

unexpected indents

Console ⌧
<terminated> C:\Users\A\workspace\My project\Tests.py
```
    File "C:\Users\A\workspace\My project\Tests.py", line 9
      print (k)
      ^
IndentationError: unexpected indent
```

Figure 13.4: An indentation error is detected at the last line before the print command.

This time the Python interpreter detected an **indentation error**. An *indentation error* is another kind of syntax error that happens due to the incorrect usage of blank space. In this case, the print command is not part of any loop, conditional, class or function. Therefore, it should not be indented.

Correct this error by finding and deleting the improper blank space, and finally you have managed to correct the whole block which looks as follows.

```
name = 'John'
if name == 'John':
    print('Your name is John')

i = 5
j = 15
k = ((i*j) + (j+i))

print(k)
```

Finally, we get an output free of errors:

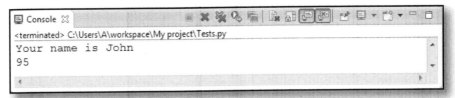

Figure 13.5: Generated output after correcting all syntax errors.

At this point, you have made sure that the code doesn't have any syntax errors.

> **Tip**: An output that is generated without errors is an indication that there are no syntax error in the code. However, there may be a different kind of errors that cannot be detected by computers, but instead need to be noticed by a human being.

QUESTIONS FOR REVIEW

1. What is the order that the interpreter checks for syntax errors?
   a. Checking classes, functions, and then variables.
   b. Checking from bottom lines to top.
   c. Checking from top lines to bottom.
   d. There is no specific order.

2. What is true about blank space in Python?
   a. It is always crucial.
   b. It is always ignored.
   c. It is ignored only if no more than four blank spaces are used.
   d. It is only crucial for indentation purposes.

LAB ACTIVITY

The following code is supposed to print all the elements of the string "John" one by one:

```
for i inside "John":
print i
```

However, the code contains two syntax errors. Try to debug them and provide the correct code.

LAB SOLUTION

```
for i in "John":
    print(i)
```

And here is the output:

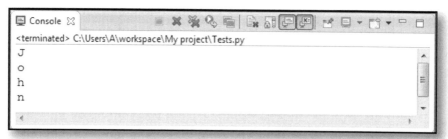

Figure 13.6: String elements printed out after the code has been debugged.

13.2 DEALING WITH ERRORS AT RUNTIME

In this section we will be looking at how to find and debug **runtime errors**.

A *runtime error* is an error in programming logic or arithmetic that is detected during the execution or **running time** of the code. The *run time itself is the period during which the program is executing.*

To better understand the concept, we will be looking at an example:

```
first = 1
second = 2
third = 3
more = input("What is the extra value? ")

total = first+seocnd+third+more
print(total)
```

In this code, we are assigning some number values to the first three variables. Then we create another user input variable that gets whatever values the user inputs when the program runs. In the last line, we calculate the sum of all the four values and print it out.

At first sight, the code looks correct. Even if you run it, everything will look in place and you will get this initial output:

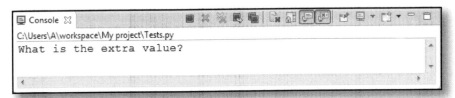

Figure 13.7: Output waiting for the user input.

At this point the last two lines of the code have not been run yet because the program is waiting for the user to input a value. We are still at *run time*. If we input a number value after the question, we are going to get an error:

```
Console ⬚                                    ✖ ✖ ◐ ▤ | ▣ ▣ ▣ ▣ | ▱ ▤ ▾ ▱ ▾ ▱ ▫
<terminated> C:\Users\A\workspace\My project\Tests.py
What is the extra value? 4
Traceback (most recent call last):
  File "C:\Users\A\workspace\My project\Tests.py", line 6, in <module>
    total = first+seocnd+third+more
NameError: name 'seocnd' is not defined
```

Figure 13.8: Error occurring at run time highlighting a not
defined variable.

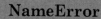

NameError

 The type of the *run time* error here
is **NameError** which indicates that the code contains a name
that has not been defined.

In this case, this undefined name is "seocnd" which has been intentionally
mistyped. Now, you should trace the error by looking up the line (line 6,
in this case) where it has occurred. Then correct it as follows and run the
code again:

```
first = 1
second = 2
third = 3
more = input("What is the extra value? ")

total = first+second+third+more
print(total)
```

You will again be prompted to input the extra value. After you do so, you
will get another run time error:

```
Console ⬚                                    ✖ ✖ ◐ ▤ | ▣ ▣ ▣ ▣ | ▱ ▤ ▾ ▱ ▾ ▱ ▫
<terminated> C:\Users\A\workspace\My project\Tests.py
What is the extra value? 4
Traceback (most recent call last):
  File "C:\Users\A\workspace\My project\Tests.py", line 6, in <module>
    total = first+second+third+more
TypeError: unsupported operand type(s) for +: 'int' and 'str'
```

Figure 13.9: Error occurring at run time highlighting an unsupported operand type.

In this case, you have run into another type
of run time error: a **TypeError**. When the

TypeError

program is trying to make the sum of the four variables, it encounters a problem.

> The *TypeError* is letting you know that an integer and a string cannot be added together.

If you are wondering where the string came from, remember that the *input()* function takes a string input by default. Therefore, even if you type in a number (4 in this case), that number will be used as a string by Python. You should explicitly declare that the input be taken as a number such as an integer. To do that, correct the code as follows:

```
first = 1
second = 2
third = 3
more = int(input("What is the extra value?
"))

total = first+second+third+more
print(total)
```

Notice that we added the *int()* function before *input()*. This will convert any number input to an integer. If you run the code this time, you will get a result that is free of errors:

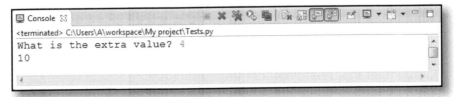

Figure 13.10: Generated output after all run time errors have been debugged.

As you see, this time you got what you were looking for. After you input 4, the program returned the total sum of (1+2+3+4) which is 10.

At this point, assisted by the interpreter, you have debugged all the run time errors that occurred as you were running your code.

1. What is *a run time* error?
   a. An error in programming logic or arithmetic that is detected at run time.
   b. An error in programming logic or arithmetic that is detected after run time.
   c. An error in programming logic or arithmetic that is detected before run time.
   d. None of the above.

2. Why does a *run time* error occur when the user enters a number as defined by the *input()* function?
   a. The number has to be defined first.
   b. The number is too big.
   c. The number has to be put inside quotes.
   d. The number is actually a string.

 LAB ACTIVITY

The following code is supposed to ask the user for their first and last names. Then it will store that data into a dictionary and print out the dictionary content. However, the code contains *run time* errors that prevent it from running successfully. Try to debug it.

```
names = {}
first = input("Enter your first name: ")
last = input("Enter your last name: ")
names.append(first, last)
print (names)
```

LAB SOLUTION

```
names = {}
first = input("Enter your first name: ")
last = input("Enter your last name: ")
names[first]= last
print (names)
```

And this is the output:

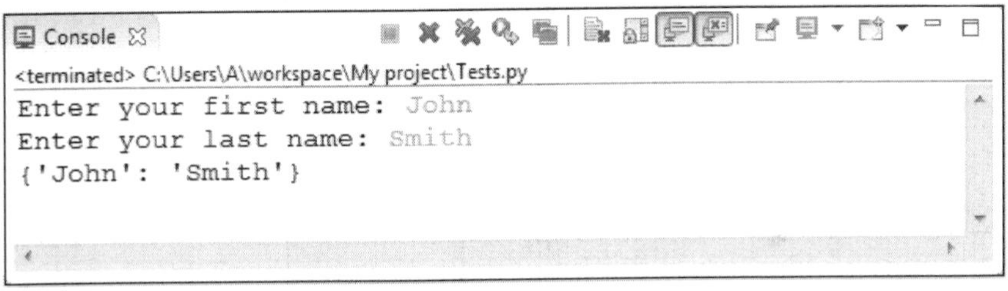

Figure 13.11: Data stored successfully inside the dictionary after the code has been debugged.

In this lab, your task is to debug a basic shell of a program.

You will find below this text three blocks of code named "create_database. py", "guestbook.py" and "users.py". Copy each of the three blocks into three separate Python scripts and name them using their respective names. The "create_database.py" has no issues within it, just run the code first to create the database. There are some bugs and problems within the other two scripts, and your task is to discover and eliminate those bugs.

"Users.py" is included in the "guestbook.py" script via the *import* command. Running "users.py" will do absolutely nothing. The important thing is to run "guestbook.py" and see the errors.

This is just a shell of a program, and currently only supports logging in and registering. If you wish to, you can build on this shell and continue with your programming, and keep learning based on what is provided within this lab.

```python
#create_database.py

import sqlite3
db = sqlite3.connect('guestbook.db')
db.execute('create table users (id INTEGER
PRIMARY KEY autoincrement, username text,
password text, date_joined int)')
db.execute('create table posts (id INTEGER
PRIMARY KEY autoincrement, poster_id int, title
text, body text, time_posted int)')
db.commit()
db.close()
import users
def display_menu():
    print('1: Login')
    print('2: Register')
    if users.is_logged_in == True:
        print('3: Post Comment')
    print('9: Exit')
```

```
    choice = input('Enter the number of where
you want to go: ')
    check_choice(choice)

#guestbook.py
def check_choice(choice):
    if choice.isdigit():
        choice = int(choice)
        if choice == 1:
            users.login()
            display_menu()
        elif choice == 2:
            users.register()
            display_menu()
        elif choice == 3:
            pass
        elif choice == 9:
            pass
        else:
            print('Please choose a correct
option')
            display_menu()
    else:
        print('Please choose a correct option')
        display_menu()
display_menu()

#users.py
import sqlite3
db = sqlite3.connect('guestbook.db')
is_logged_in = False
user_id = 0 # 0 means not set / not logged in.

def register():
    username = input('Please enter a username:
')
    if username_available(username) == True :
        import hashlib, time
        password = input('Please enter a
password: ').encode('utf_8')
        encrypted = hashlib.sha256()
```

```python
        encrypted.update(password)
        newpass = encrypted.hexdigest()

        currenttime = int(time.time())
        db.execute('insert into users
(username, password, date_joined) values
(?,?,?)',(username,newpass, currenttime))
        db.commit()
        print('You have been added to the user
database')
        return True
    else:
        print('Unfortunately, that username is
already taken. Please try again')
        register()
def login():
    username = input('Please enter your
username: ')
    if username_available(username) == False:
#if it is taken, then it must exist.
        import hashlib
        password = input('Please enter your
password: ').encode('utf_8')
        encrypted = hashlib.sha256()
        encrypted.update(password)
        newpass = encrypted.hexdigest()

        db.row_factory = sqlite3.Row
        row = db.execute('select id from
users where username = ? and password = ?',
(username, newpass))
        if row is None:
            print('Sorry, that password doesn\'
match the username')
        else:
            user_id = row.fetchone()['id']
            is_logged_in = True
    else:
        print('That user doesn\'t exist.
Register it?')
def logout():
```

```
    pass
def username_available(username):
    db.row_factory = sqlite3.Row
    row = db.execute('select id from users
WHERE username = ?',(username,))

    if row.fetchone() is None:
        return True
    else:
        return False
```

Lab Solution

The debugged and corrected code for the three
scripts is as follows:

```
#create_database.py

import sqlite3
db = sqlite3.connect('guestbook.db')
db.execute('create table if not exists users
(id INTEGER PRIMARY KEY autoincrement, username
text, password text, date_joined int)')
db.execute('create table if not exists posts
(id INTEGER PRIMARY KEY autoincrement, poster_
id int, title text, body text, time_posted
int)')
db.commit()
db.close()

#guestbook.py

import users
def display_menu():
    print('1: Login')
    print('2: Register')
    if users.is_logged_in == True:
        print('3: Post Comment')
    print('9: Exit')
    choice = input('Enter the number of where
```

```
you want to go: ')
    check_choice(choice)

def check_choice(choice):
    if choice.isdigit():
        choice = int(choice)
        if choice == 1:
            users.login()
            display_menu()
        elif choice == 2:
            users.register()
            display_menu()
        elif choice == 3:
            pass
        elif choice == 9:
            pass
        else:
            print('Please choose a correct
option')
            display_menu()
    else:
        print('Please choose a correct option')
        display_menu()
display_menu()

#users.py

import sqlite3
db = sqlite3.connect('guestbook.db')
is_logged_in = False
user_id = 0 # 0 means not set / not logged in.

def register():
    username = input('Please enter a username:
')
    if username_available(username) == True :
        import hashlib, time
        password = input('Please enter a
password: ').encode('utf_8')
        encrypted = hashlib.sha256()
        encrypted.update(password)
```

```
        newpass = encrypted.hexdigest()

        currenttime = int(time.time())
        db.execute('insert into users
(username, password, date_joined) values
(?,?,?)',(username,newpass, currenttime))
        db.commit()
        print('You have been added to the user
database')
        return True
    else:
        print('Unfortunately, that username is
already taken. Please try again')
        register()
def login():
    username = input('Please enter your
username: ')
    if username_available(username) == False:
#if it is taken, then it must exist.
        import hashlib
        password = input('Please enter your
password: ').encode('utf_8')
        encrypted = hashlib.sha256()
        encrypted.update(password)
        newpass = encrypted.hexdigest()

        db.row_factory = sqlite3.Row
        row = db.execute('select id from
users where username = ? and password = ?',
(username, newpass))
        if row is None:
            print('Sorry, that password doesn\'
match the username')
        else:
            user_id = row.fetchone()['id']
            is_logged_in = True
    else:
        print('That user doesn\'t exist.
Register it?')
def logout():
    pass
```

```
def username_available(username):
    db.row_factory = sqlite3.Row
    row = db.execute('select id from users
WHERE username = ?',(username,))

    if row.fetchone() is None:
        return True
    else:
        return False
```

After you run the correct code, by executing "create_database.py" first, and then "guestbook.py", you will get this output:

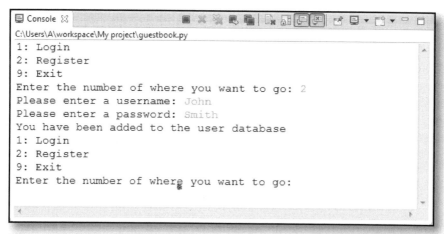

Figure 13.12: Output after running the corrected code of "create_database.py" and "guestbook.py".

CHAPTER SUMMARY

In this chapter you learned how to detect syntax errors, how to find their exact or approximate location in the lines of code of the script, and how to correct the errors using the interpreter hints as a guide.

You were introduced to run time errors, when and where they occur and how to free your code of them.

This brings you to the end of our Python for Beginners book. If before reading this book, you had never programmed before in your life, you should now feel confident enough to do so. With some effort, you can start building your own programs that go beyond the examples and the exercises we have gone through this book in terms of size and complexity.

If before reading this book, you were an already experienced programmer who wanted to expand your programming skills with Python, you should now understand the advantages of this language as compared to other languages. Compared to other languages, Python code is much more readable, mainly boosted by its indentation feature. This readability is complemented by Python's brevity. Python requires fewer lines of code to solve a programming problem than other languages.

There are many ways you can use Python. Python can be used in web development along with frameworks like Django and TurboGears, to name a few.

Python can be used as a tool to access databases such as MySQL, Oracle, and PostgreSQL.

Even though in this chapter we learned only scripting, it is worth mentioning that you can build your own graphical user interface program using Python libraries such as the built-in Tkinter. With a bit of learning you can easily associate your scripts with buttons, text boxes and other tools of desktop graphical programs.

Its powerful scripting capabilities make Python a widely used language for scientific calculations in areas such as physics and bioinformatics. Python also provides support for low-level network programming via Twisted Python, a network programming framework designed to work with Python.

Python is also often used as a support language for software developers, for build control and management, testing, and in many other ways. Gaming is not left behind. Through PyGame or PyKyra frameworks, you can create many types of commercial and hobby games.

No matter what the area of your interest is, you should now be able to kick-start your own real program using the skills you learned in this book.

FINAL QUESTIONS FOR REVIEW

1. What data types are designed to store sequences?
   a. Classes and functions.
   b. Libraries.
   c. Lists, tuples and dictionaries.
   d. Strings.

2. Which expression will generate a syntax error?
   a. if
   b. else
   c. else if
   d. elif

3. What is at the core of a loop?
   a. Iteration.
   b. Condition.
   c. Modification.
   d. Encapsulation.

4. What is not true about the range() function?
   a. It generates a list.
   b. It is used to iterate over sequences of numbers.
   c. It allows the programmer to define the step of a for loop.
   d. Range (10) is a sequence from one to 10.

5. What tool allows the interaction between an end user and a program?
   a. A cautious object-oriented programming.
   b. A friendly graphical interface.
   c. An input() function.
   d. PyDev module of Eclipse.

6. What is true about splitting and joining strings?
   a. A string can be split through several strings using the split() function.
   b. Several strings can be joined using the join() function.
   c. Several lists can be joined to a string using the join() function.
   d. List elements can be joined to a string using the join() function.

7. What is not true about custom functions?
   a. Functions are used when an action is meant to be performed multiple times.

b. You can define a function in any Python script.

c. You can call a function that has been defined in another script.

d. The number of arguments has to be the same as the number of parameters.

8. What would be the best scenario for using classes?

a. When you want to repeat the same calculations, but using different values.

b. When you want to create a prototype object and call object instances afterwards.

c. When the actions you want to perform are too many for one function to handle.

d. When you want to keep your custom functions organized.

9. What is not true about class methods?

a. A method is an initializer of a class.

b. A method is a function defined within a class.

c. A method can be called by referencing it to its class.

d. A method can take parameters and arguments just like a function.

10. What would you use to write data to a binary file?

a. The file handling library.

b. An open() function with a wb parameter.

c. An open() function with a w parameter.

d. The sqlite3 library.

11. What is true about the sqlite3 library?

a. It is the only available library that enables database interaction.

b. It enables SQL operations within Python.

c. It is a built-in Python module.

d. It is used to pop up database tables in the form of windows.

12. What is an incorrect way of enabling the use of the function called custom() in the module sample.py?

a. import sample

b. import sample.py

c. from sample import *

d. from sample import custom

13. Which of the following is not a module/library?

a. slqite3

b. os

c. datetime

d. path

14. Which of the following statements is wrong?
    a. Using a good interpreter can help detect errors.
    b. Using a Python interpreter extension may enable Python code debugging.
    c. Using try and except is a way to handle errors.
    d. There is no specific way to handle errors.

15. What is not an error type in Python?
    a. IOError
    b. NameError
    c. TypeError
    d. IterationError

ANSWER KEY: PYTHON FOR BEGINNERS

Chapter 1.1 Acquiring the tools

1. Which of the following is needed to write and run a simple Python program such as the one created in this chapter?
Answer: c. Python.

2. Which of the following statements is true?
Answer: c. Eclipse is just an optional platform that helps users to work with Python.

Chapter 1.2 Hello World in Python

1. What does the *print* command do?
Answer: b. Displays some text on the screen.

2. What is not meant by "running the program"?
Answer: a. Saving the written program inside Eclipse.

Chapter 2: The Basics

1. Let's say we have assigned a value to variable *a* as *a = 1*
Which of the following codes would print out the variable's assigned value?
Answer: c. print (a)

2. Which of the following is not a data type in Python?
Answer: b. Decimal

3. Which of the following is not a correct declaration in Python?
Answer: b. b={1,2,3}

4. Which of the following would be a correct order of execution of arithmetic operators, assuming there are no parentheses in the expression?
Answer: b. Roots, multiplication, addition

5. What is not true about comments?
Answer: a: Comments are lines of code that automatically generate descriptions.

Chapter 3: Conditionals

1. Which of the following is a correctly written expression?
Answer: b. if a == b:
           Print("Yes")

2. What is not true about *elif*?
Answer: b. *Elif* is a substitute of the switch function.

3. What happens when none of the conditions are true in a conditional block?
Answer: a. The action under else is executed.

4. How would you write a code that prints "Greater" if *a* is greater than *b*, and "Less or equal" if *a* is less than or equal to *b*, using the *inline if* statement?
Answer: c. a, b = 10,20
        print ("Less or equal " if a <= b else "Greater")

Chapter 4: Looping

1. What would the following code do when executed?
Answer: c. Print out even numbers that fall between zero and 100.

2. What does the range functionality do?
Answer: a. Generates a list.

3. The *for* loop is commonly used to:
Answer: c. Iterate through lists, tuples and strings.

4. What is true about *try* and *except*?
Answer: b. The expression under *except* is executed when the expression under *try* experiences an error.

5. What happens when the condition above the break code line is not met?
Answer: b. The line under break is not executed.

Chapter 5: Lists

1. What is true about negative indexing?
Answer: a. It provides an easy method to enumerate list elements starting from the end.

2. What would the code below do if executed?
   Answer: c. Print out false.

3. How would you delete element *a* from list *b*?
   Answer: c. del b[a]

4. Number *3* is missing from list *a = [1,2,4,5]* we need to add it again.
   There are different methods of adding number 3 to its proper position
   (after number 2) inside the list. Which of these methods would be an
   incorrect method of adding the number in its proper position?
   Answer: d. a.insert(3)
         a.sort()

Chapter 6: Receiving Inputs

1. When running the following code:

```
list = [1,2,3]
a = input('Add a number to the list: ')
list.append(a)
print (list)
```

the user is prompted to type in a number. If the user types in "4", what
would the program generate?
Answer: d. [1, 2, 3, '4']

2. When running the following code:

```
list = [1,2,3]
a = input('Add a number to the list: ')
list.append(int(a))
print (list)
```

the user is prompted to type in a number. If the user types in "4", what
would the program generate?
Answer: b. [1,2,3,4]

3. Which of the following is true?
Answer: c. The generated list in question 2 contains only number
elements.

Chapter 7: Predifined String Functions

1. Which of the structures best represents the following code?
Answer: a. object.method()

2. What does the second line of the following code do?
   Answer: d. It assigns the altered value of variable *a* to variable *c*.
3. What does the *split()* method return?
   Answer: c. A list.

4. What does the *join()* method return?
   Answer: b. A string.

Chapter 8: Custom Functions

1. Which of the following is a correct way of defining a custom function?
   Answer: a. def function():
   return

2. What is not true about functions?
   Answer: d. Functions cannot contain other functions inside them.

3. What is not true about variable scope and functions?
   Answer: a. Global variables cannot be used inside a function.

Chapter 9.1: Overview of classes and objects.

1. Which of the following best describes a class?
   Answer: d. A prototype with methods within it.

2. What is a class method?
   Answer: b. A function.

Chapter 9.2: Using "class"

1. How do you start writing a class?
   Answer: a. class classname:

2. What would you do to get an output from a defined class?
   Answer b: call a class instance.

Chapter 9.3: Using Methods

1. Which of the following is not a keyword in Python?
   Answer: a. self

2. What is the correct method of calling a class instance method?
   Answer: a. class().method()

Chapter 9.4: Using Object Data

1. What would "*kwargs" indicate when passed as a parameter of a class?
   Answer: a. Method parameters will be stored in a dictionary called "kwargs".

2. In the previous example, what does the get_vars() method do?
   Answer: c. It returns the corresponding value of a dictionary key.

Chapter 9.5: Inheritance

1. When would you use inheritance?
   Answer: d. When some of the methods of a class you want to create are contained in an existing class.

2. How would you start writing the class *child* that is inherited from the class *parent*?
   Answer: d. class child(parent)

Chapter 10: File Handling

1. What does the following code do?

```
file = open("Sections.txt")
for i in file:
    print (i)
```

   Answer: b. Prints out the content of "Sections.txt" on a line by line basis.

2. Why do we set a big buffer size number?
   Answer: a. To have the code run more quickly.

3. What is not true about the buffer technique?
   Answer: d. It works better with text files.

Chapter 11.1: Creating the Database

1. What does the *import sqlite3* command do?
   Answer: c. Imports a library that is able to handle interactions with a database.

2. What argument does the *execute()* method take?
   Answer: d. SQL code.

Chapter 11.2: Inserting and Updating Records

1. Which of the following is not a SQL keyword?
   Answer: d. execute()

2. What would you do to change an existing record from a table?
   Answer: a. Use the *update* keyword.

Chapter 11.3: Retrieving and Deleting Records

1. What command do we use to retrieve database records?
   Answer: a. select

2. Why would we use a dictionary when retrieving records from a database?
   Answer: d. To have the record values attached to their field names.

Chapter 12.1: Using Standard Libraries

1. What is the first step when you want to use a library inside Python?
   Answer: b. Import the library

2. Which of the following would correctly print out the current date and time?
   Answer: d. print (datetime.datetime.now())

Chapter 12.2: Creating a module

1. What is not true about modules?
   Answer: d. Choosing to work with modules is just a matter of style.

2. What does the following line of code from the previous example do?
   Answer: d. It calls the function *greeting()* contained in *SampleModule*.

Chapter 13.1: Dealing with Syntax Errors

1. What is the order that the interpreter checks for syntax errors?
   Answer: c. Checking from top lines to bottom.

2. What is true about blank space in Python?
   Answer: d. It is only crucial for indentation purposes.

Chapter 13.2: Dealing with Errors at Runtime

1. What is a run time error?
   Answer: a. An error in programming logic or arithmetic that must be detected at run time.

2. Why does a run time error occur when the user enters a number as defined by the *input()* function?
   Answer: d. The number is actually a string.

Final Quiz

1. What data types are designed to store sequences?
   Answer: c. Lists, tuples and dictionaries.

2. Which expression will generate a syntax error?
   Answer: c. else if

3. What is at the core of a loop?
   Answer: a. Iteration

4. What is not true about the *range()* function?
   Answer: d. *Range(10)* is a sequence from one to 10

5. What tool allows the interaction between an end user and a program?
   Answer: c. An *input()* function.

6. What is true about splitting and joining strings?
   Answer: d. List elements can be joined to a string using the *join()* function.

7. What is not true about custom functions?
   Answer: d. The number of arguments has to be the same as the number of parameters.

8. What would be the best scenario for using classes?
   Answer: b. When you want to create a prototype object and call object instances afterwards.

9. What is not true about class methods?
   Answer: a. A method is an initializer of a class.

10. What would you use to write data to a binary file?
    Answer: b. An *open()* function with a *wb* parameter.

11. What is true about the *sqlite3* library?
    Answer b. It enables SQL operations within Python.

12. What is an incorrect way of enabling the use of the function called custom() in the module sample.py?
    Answer: b. import sample.py

13. Which of the following is not a module/library?
    Answer: d. path

14. Which of the following statements is wrong?
    Answer: d. There is no specific way to handle errors.

15. What is not an error in Python?
    Answer d. IterationError

Appendix

Terminology	Description
API	This abbreviation means Application Programming Interface. It is a software-to-software interface that specifies how programmers can make their own software access and interact with the features and capabilities of another software. For example, by using an API to interact with an established email software platform, programmers can build email capabilities into any software they develop.
Append()	A method that adds an object to the end of a container-type object.
Argument	A value passed to the function when the function is called. Arguments are passed by assignment (object reference).
AttributeError	An error raised when an attribute reference or assignment fails.
Bitwise operator	An operator that evaluates two or more expressions.
Break	A program statement that breaks out of the smallest enclosing of a for or while loop.
Boolean	A data type with only two possible values: "true" or "false".
Buffer	A technique to access text files based on groups of text instead of bits.
Casting	The process of converting one data type to another.
Class	A construct that is used to define a distinct type of data structure.
class	A keyword that precedes the name of the class that is being created.
Class variable	A variable defined inside a class of which a single copy exists regardless of the number of instances of that class.

Terminology	Description
Collection	Python collections are a group of specialized container objects that are alternatives to Python's general purpose built-in containers – dict, list, set, and tuple. Some examples of Python colections are ChainMap, OrderedDict, UserList, UserString, etc.
Command prompt	An interface for users of an operating system to access the services of a kernel (such as Windows).
Comment	Descriptive text wrapped using certain syntax with the aim to be ignored by the interpreter while executing.
Conditional	A statement block performing actions dependent on the evaluation of certain conditions.
connect()	A sqlite3 library method that establishes a connection with a database and allows the execution of SQL statements on that database.
Constructor	A special type of function called to create an object and initialize its member variables.
container	A data structure that holds or stores objects. (A container is itself an object.) Generally, containers provide a way to access the contained objects and to iterate over them. Python has two generic container type objects – mappings and sequences.
continue	A statement that continues the next iteration of the loop.
Cursor	An object that holds data that has a database format.
Data member	A class variable or an instance variable that holds data associated with a class and its objects.
Database	A system of an organized collection of information that can be accessed quickly by computer programs.
datetime	A library that supports manipulations of time and date variables.
Debug	The process of finding and removing program errors.
def	A keyword used in a statement that creates a function object, assigns it a name and, optionally, lists the arguments that are to be passed to the function.

Terminology	Description
Dictionary	A Python built-in container of unordered values accessed by key rather than by index.
Dictionary key	One of two elements of a dictionary pair that is used to find its corresponding value.
Dictionary value	One of two elements of a dictionary pair that is accessed through its corresponding key.
Django	A Python Web framework that encourages rapid development and clean, pragmatic design.
Encapsulation	In programming, this is a mechanism for restricting access to some of the object's components.
Eclipse	A platform where you can write, edit, debug and run code such as Python.
Elif	A keyword similar to else with the difference that it can be used multiple times. Else can only be used once.
Else	A keyword that triggers execution of the indented block of code following the keyword if the previous conditional clauses are not met.
Enumerate	A method that returns a sequence, an iterator, or some other object which supports iteration.
except	A clause that displays an error if the execution of the code under the try clause results in an error.
execute()	A sqlite3 library method that enables the execution of SQL code inside Python.
Exception	An error detected during execution that is not unconditionally fatal.
finally	A clause that is executed before leaving the try statement, whether an exception has occurred or not.
Float	A numeric data type that stores decimal values.
For loop	A loop commonly used to iterate through container data types.
Function	A named section of a program that performs a specific task using different inputs.
getattr()	A function used to fetch an attribute from an object, using a string object instead of an identifier.

Terminology	Description
Global variable	Variable declared outside a function and that can be used anywhere inside the script.
Hash value	A unique number generated by a formula from a string of text. It is generated in such a way that it is highly unlikely that some other text will produce the same hash value. A hash value is also called a message digest or simply a hash.
hashable	An object is hashable if it has a hash value which never changes during its lifetime. Hashable objects which compare equal must have the same hash value. Hashability makes an object usable as a dictionary key and a set member, because dictionaries and sets use the hash value internally.
If	A keyword introducing a conditional clause.
import	A command preceded by a library name that enables the functionality of that library within the current script.
Indentation	Blank spacing used to identify where blocks of code begin and end.
Inheritance	A transfer of the characteristics of one class (the base or superclass) to another class (the derived class or the subclass).
Initiation	The process that signals the creation of a class.
Inline if	A method for writing conditional blocks in a single line.
input()	A built-in or library function that stores user input.
int()	A built-in or library function that converts a number or a string to an integer.
Instance	A specific realization of any object.
Instance variable	A variable that is defined inside a class, for which each object of the class has a separate copy or instance.
Integer	A set of negative and positive whole numbers and zero.
Interpreter	A computer program that performs instructions written in a programming language.

Terminology	Description
IOError	An error raised when an I/O operation fails for an I/O-related reason.
iterable	An object capable of returning its objects (sometimes referred to as its members or its elements) one at a time.
Iteration	A general term for successively taking each item of a container, one after another. It also refers to repeatedly executing, a fixed number of times or until a certain condition is met.
Indentation error	An error caused by improper or incorrect indentation.
Java Runtime Environment	A software development environment that provides the libraries and components to run applets and applications written in the Java programming language.
join()	A method that forms a string from the elements of a container.
Keyword	A word that cannot be used by a programmer to name variables, functions, etc. because that word is already used by the programming language.
kwargs	A special function parameter enabling an arbitrary number of arguments to be passed to a function.
len	A method that returns the number of objects in a container.
Library	A set of Python scripts or modules that contain already-made functions used for specialized operations.
Linux	An open source computer operating system modeled on Unix.
List	One of the six sequence data types of Python. A list stores a sequence of comma-separated objects (items) between square brackets. Lists are mutable.
Local variable	Variable declared inside a function and meant to be used only inside that function.
Loop	A block of indented instructions that is continually repeated until a certain condition is reached.

Terminology	Description
Mapping	One of Python's two generic container type objects (the other being sequences). Mapping objects map hashable values to the arbitrary objects contained in it. Mappings are mutable objects. The only mapping object in Python is the dictionary.
Method	A function that is attached to and acts upon a specific object. Methods are triggered by a call expression.
Module	A file of scripts that can be imported into other scripts.
MySQL	An open-source relational database management system that runs as a server providing multi-user access to a number of databases.
NameError	An error caused when the name of a variable, function, class, etc. has not been defined is used inside the script.
Negative indexing	Indexing of members of a container object starting with an index of -1 (for the last or rightmost element) and increasing from right to left.
now()	A datetime library function that returns the current date and time.
Object	A location in memory having a value and referenced by an identifier.
open()	A function used to access disk files from within Python.
Operand	A quantity on which an operation is performed.
Oracle Database	An object-relational database management system produced and marketed by Oracle Corporation.
Parameter	A special kind of variable, used in a function to refer to one of the pieces of data provided as input to the function.
path	A sys module method that returns the search path for modules.
Positive indexing	Indexing of object elements starting with zero (for the first element) and increasing from left to right.

Terminology	Description
PostgreSQL	An open source object-relational database management system with an emphasis on extensibility and standards compliance.
Print	A built-in function that evaluates expressions and writes the resulting object to standard output.
PyDev	A third-party Integrated Development Environment plug-in for Eclipse used for programming in Python and which supports code refactoring, graphical debugging, code analysis and many other features.
PyGame	A cross-platform set of Python modules designed for writing video games
PyKyra	A game development framework for Python.
Python	A powerful dynamic programming language that is used in a wide variety of application domains.
range	A built-in function that generates arithmetic progressions. It does not generate a list object. It is simply an object which returns the successive items of the desired sequence when you iterate over it.
record	Also called a row or a tuple. a record is a set of data that has the same structure in the table.
return	A command that passes the output of the function to the calling function.
row	Also called a record or a tuple, this is a set of data that has the same record structure as the table.
row_factory	A sqlite3 library method that enables the retrieval of the database data in form of a Python dictionary.
Run	A command to execute a computer program.
Runtime	The period during which a program is executing.
self	The instance object automatically passed to the class instance's method when called.

Terminology	Description
sequence	A positionally ordered collection of other objects. Sequences maintain a left-to-right order among its members. The members of a sequence are stored and fetched by their relative positions. The six sequence types of Python are: strings, Unicode strings, lists, tuples, buffers, and xrange objects. A sequence is also one of Python's two generic container types, the other being mappings.
slice notation	A method of indicating a portion (substring) of a string. In its most common form, slice notation requires two integers separated by a colon [a:b] where the leftmost integer is a starting index and the rightmost integer is the ending index. The substring begins with the character at index a and continues up to but does not include the character at position b. The length of the substring is b-a.
split()	A method of the string object that splits a string and generates a list whose members are the split parts of the string.
SQL	Structured Query Language. A special-purpose programming language designed for managing data in relational database management systems.
sqlite3	A C library that allows Python programs to interact with a light-weight disk-based database. No server separate process is required. A non-standard variant of the SQL is used to access the database.
Statement	An instruction in a computer program.
Step (iteration)	A number that defines the intensity at which the iteration loop accesses sequence elements.
str()	A built-in function that converts numbers to strings.
String	One of the six sequence data types of Python. A string stores an ASCII or UTF-8 sequence of comma-separated objects (items) between single or double-quotation marks. Strings are mutable.
String formatting	A set of procedures for manipulating strings.
Superclass	A class whose characteristics have been inherited by another class, the subclass.

Terminology	Description
Syntax	Grammatical rules and structural patterns governing the ordered use of appropriate words and symbols for writing code.
Syntax error	An error caused due to incorrectly used syntax.
sys	A module that supports functions that interact with the interpreter.
Terminal	An interface for users of an operating system to access the services of a kernel (Linux).
Tkinter	A library that supports the creation of standard graphical user interfaces within Python.
Truth table	A diagram in rows and columns showing how the truth or falsity of a proposition varies with that of its components.
try	A clause that allows the execution of its indented statement block if no errors occur.
Tuple (databases)	Also called a record or a row, a tuple is a set of data that has the same structure in the table.
Tuple (Python)	One of the six sequence data types of Python. A tuple stores a sequence of comma-separated objects (items) between parentheses. Tuples are immutable.
Turbo Gears	Web framework integrating several Python projects.
Twisted Python	An event-driven network programming framework written in Python.
TypeError	An error caused when an operand is applied to an inappropriate data type. For example, concatenating a string and a number.
Variable	A symbolic name associated with a memory storage location which contains a value.
Variable scope	A quality of a variable that determines if a variable is global or local.
While loop	A loop commonly used to execute statements until a condition is met.
__init__	A constructor when an instance of a class is created.

You've Read the Book -
Now Take the Online Course From the Author

50% DISCOUNT

To all of our readers, we're offering our LearnToProgram courses at 50% off. These are courses that include hours of <u>video instruction</u>, various <u>code samples</u> and applicable <u>lab exercises</u>. You'll watch as the author develops the code right in front of you while you gain skills you can immediately apply to your projects.

All courses are available at: **https://academy.learntoprogram.tv/directory/**.

To apply your Reader's Discount, go to any course of your choosing, click to enroll and then select "Redeem Coupon."

Use coupon code: **BOOK**

Courses:	Direct Link: https://academy.learntoprogram.tv/ ...
AJAX Development	course/ajax-tutorial-training/
Android for Beginners	course/android-programming-development-for-beginners/
C Prgm. for Beginners	course/learn-c-programming/
CSS Dev. (with CSS3!)	course/learn-css-development/
Design for Coders	course/photoshop-cs6-training-for-coders/
HTML5 Mobile App Dev. with PhoneGap	course/html5-mobile-app-development-phonegap/
HTML & CSS for Beginners	course/html-css-for-beginners/
iOS5 Dev. for Beginners	course/ios-iphone-ipad-development-for-beginners/
Javascript for Beginners	course/javascript-for-beginners/
jQuery for Beginners	course/learn-jquery-for-beginners/
Objective C for Beginners	course/objective-c-for-beginners/
Photoshop for Beginners	course/photoshop-cs6-training-for-coders/
PHP/MySQL for Beginners	course/learn-php-mysql-for-beginners/
Python for Beginners	course/python-for-beginners/
SQL DB for Beginners	course/sql-database-for-beginners/
User Exp. Design	course/user-experience-design-fundamentals/

4755621R00128

Printed in Great Britain
by Amazon.co.uk, Ltd.,
Marston Gate.